THE PATHFINDER

Title: Break Those Damn Rules
Author: Lynn Erasmus

Publisher: LYNNERASMUS Ltd.
(trading as) The Pathfinder

Location: United Kingdom

Year: 2020

FORWARD

"I absolutely love this book! I picked it up and I could not put it down until it was finished.
It is incredibly written, she is such a great storyteller. It is light-hearted, but filled with wisdom.

I loved how each Chapter leads you into the next, taking you on a journey of her life and written in such a pleasant and relatable manner. It is so honest and raw.
Her opinions might not be very popular, but it's refreshing to hear.

I love her incredible optimism and her openness to share her story with us.
Her life lessons on how we can teach ourselves to live differently, without taking anything away from who we are.

I think every women and person should read this.
It is a spiritual journey and you take what works for you. She is a modern day women and is unapologetically herself.
She inspired me so much, thank you."
Ellen Fischat, CEO - Storyroom, #Inspiring50
Ambassador

DEDICATION

This book is dedicated to my darling children and husband. My love and gratitude for this precious trio has no bounds. Thank you husband for forcing me to purge my thoughts, encouraging me when I wanted to give up and not complaining about my obsessive, compulsive desire to write and rewrite the book at three in the morning – keeping me energised with coffee and looking after the children to give me space. A special mention to my beautiful Angels for their love and constant reassurance that all is as it should be. Also, a big thank you to my gorgeous crazy family, dear friends, business colleagues and random people I have met on social media.
You have all inspired me.

ISBN 978-1-8382788-2-3 Print
ISBN 978-1-8382788-3-0 E-Book

Any references to historical events, real people or real places are written according to the recollection of the Author's memory. Real people's names have been changed to protect their identities. All information in this book is given as a true reflection of the Author's account of events.

Design by Kamila Wiss
Edited by Candice Pirie

Contact:
breakthosedamnrules@gmail.com
www.lynnerasmus.com
FB @breakthosedamnrules
Instagram @breakthosedamnrules
LinkedIn: Lynn (Erasmus) van Vuuren

CONTENTS

DEAR CHILDREN

I want you to read this book with an open mind and heart. Not with pity, sadness, or anger.
I will gladly go through all the horrors in my life again if I can spare you just one of these experiences.
I know you will live your own life one day and I encourage you, above all – to truly live!
I want you to smell the flowers every day, give thanks to the Creator for all that you have and all that you are.
I want you to hold gratitude for everything in your life, big and small. I want you to never lose your childlike wonder and awe for life.
I want you to be free. If you are free in your mind, then you are free in body and spirit.
Never forget those that helped you on your journey and never be too big for the little guy.
I want you to be big enough to admit when you made a mistake and be brave my little ones.
Trust in The Universal Law
of The Creator – You are what you think you are.

Make this your tagline:

> **"Watch your thoughts, they become
> your words; watch your words, they become your actions;
> watch your actions, they become your habits; watch your
> habits, they become your character; watch your character,
> it becomes your destiny." — Lao Tzu**

I want you to never seek the approval of others, what people think of you is none of your business.
You cannot change people, you cannot make them like or love you, you can only change the way you think and feel about a person or situation.
The world truly is your oyster, and you are the captain of the ship.
You determine how your life will be.

If you do not like the way your life is going, then change it. It is that simple.
Be brave, be kind, be tenacious, and always finish what you started. It shows character and strength.
The biggest lesson your father taught me is that being gentle is not a weakness, it is a strength.
I want you to be gentle and strong.
I want you to love in abundance and not fear being hurt.
Rather apologise for doing something, than ask for permission before you do. Trust me, it is better to do something with the possibility of regret, than to not do it and always wonder 'what if'.
Do not be the 'what if' kind of person.
Take calculated risks, trust your instincts (your inner voice), that nudge, or butterflies in your stomach.
If something does not feel right, then do not do it, no matter how logical it sounds.
If something tells you not to trust a certain person or situation, walk away immediately and do not give it any further thought. I need you to remember your father's words:

"Always be kind to each other and those around you".

It is important to know your worth.
We have brought you up to be strong and confident and to know how worthy you are, but always remain kind.
I love you so much and there truly is nothing in this world or the next, that I would not do for you.
Always know how worthy, beautiful, kind, funny and strong you both are.
You are our children and God's little angels, borrowed to us for our journey on earth. You have both made me a better person and managed to bring out the shine in me.
Thank you for choosing us as your parents.

Always remember to follow your heart and live your bliss, as life is a precious gift.
It is just a game we play.
We might not always win, but we must still always play. Choose your game and play it, my loves.

With love, Mommy. Xxx

BREAK THOSE DAMN HABITS – IN 21 DAYS

Over the next few chapters, I will be sharing advice on how I overcame my bad habits with you. I learned that you need to be disciplined, determined and to see your end goal with crystal clear clarity. Your focus must be razor-sharp and your desire - as great as for life itself. Do not force it, your time will come when you want 'a better you' more than anything else in the world or to 'break those damn habits' that you can't seem to shake. If there is a single grain of doubt, then leave this section.
You will know the right time when the day arrives. You will hear the call and you will not be able to carry on with 'normal' life until you have answered.

This 21-day practical worksheet works best if you dedicate one day per instruction.
If you are anything like me, I would try to cram as many as possible into one day. That is also ok, my fellow obsessive reader, so long as you do it for 21 days as that is how long it consistently takes to break a habit. Here is to a new and better version of you.

Enjoy the book at your own leisure and use the 21-day worksheets in between days.

Big hug. You've got this! Xxx

DAY 1: WHAT DO YOU WANT IN LIFE?

Make a list of all the things you want in your life. Remember to include a few that scare you – they should be that big!
(Example)

Lynn Erasmus 13/10/2020

1. I want to lose 10kg by May 2021.
2. I want to be an International Best-Selling Author.
3. I want to be kinder and more assertive.
4. I want to be financially free by my birthday.
5. I want to travel the world and experience new cultures.

Make the list, write your name on it and date it. Hang it up on your wall - either next to your bed where you get to see it every night, or next to your bathroom mirror, so you can read it while brushing your teeth. Remember that there is no such thing as being 'greedy'. You can have it all and you should have it all. You are worthy!
It is only once you accept this fact that blessings and prosperity flow into your life.

Add one thing you are grateful for. Close your eyes and feel the joy.
Positive affirmation: "I am worthy of receiving abundance".

CHAPTER ONE
SOUTH AFRICA
(1980-)

I was born in Namibia (South West Africa), in a mining town called Tsumeb. At the time there was not much infrastructure and so I was born in an army tent. I was my dad's birthday present – born on his birthday at 9 pm. My dad said he cracked open some champagne and they celebrated my birth and his birthday together in the hospital.

I cannot even fathom it, drinking in a "hospital", with the doctor to boot. Namibia is a must-see country. Its vastness and emptiness filled with warm, dry air, surrounded by the animals and the Sahara Desert. I can understand why celebrities such as Prince Harry, Meghan Markle, Brad Pitt, and Angelina Jolie would choose to visit Namibia above any other country. Namibia is also known for some of the oldest rock paintings estimated at over 25 000 BC and the owner of a fragment of a hominoid jaw – thought to be thirteen million years old, found in the Otavi Mountains.

Back to my beautiful country, South Africa. You must at some point in your life experience it, even if only once.

It is breathtakingly beautiful.

It is wild, rough and rugged, but the sky is the bluest you will ever see and when the sun sets upon the horizon, it burns with a feverish red and orange glow and you just know, this is Africa.

It has a heartbeat like no other country I have ever been to.

Its rhythm is constant, and it is like dancing when you walk, you must keep moving, it urges you to keep going, just a little bit further. It burns with passion and heat, with anger and fear, but then the soft morning breeze strokes your face with a gentleness that makes you want to cry and your heart beats just a little bit stronger again.

How I long for my beautiful country. My heart cries for my people.

We are so robust and vibrant. We are passionate, loud, obnoxious, and proud. We are spiteful and vengeful, but in return, we love with such ferocity, it builds you up from the ground and brings you into the light. We laugh easily, and behind the scowling eyes is always a twinkle of mischief waiting to come alive. We do not accept pity from others, we are strong and resilient, and we band together under the African sky. We see opportunities in all challenges, we hustle, and can make jewellery out of your rubbish. We are versatile and kind, we share with those who have so little, but we may also take your life, for a few coins. The life expectancy for the masses is short, we live for the moment as tomorrow might never come. We take nothing for granted and we always think any other country would be better than ours.

All of this is true and untrue, at the same time.

I hope and pray that one day I can return and retire there under my beautiful African sky. But for now, I must think of the future of my children. You see, if it were just Paul and I, and we had no kids, I would never have left South Africa. I would have stayed there and kept on fighting every day to make a living and to be ever alerted to staying alive, but that would be selfish. We did the deed and had babies, and it is now our responsibility to ensure that we give them the best possible life available to them.

My husband has his British passport thanks to his beautiful mother that was born in London. She was a war baby and can remember the bombings, being separated from her parents as a little girl and living on food stamps. It was a hard time to be alive, but she endured and made it. Her Scottish ancestors were the Fergusons and Urquhart that became the Finlayson's (interesting little side note). I feel like we went full circle in our travels. South Africa – The Netherlands – Scotland. So back to Africa.

Why did we leave our beautiful country? Why do most people leave? For better opportunities and safety. Those were our main reasons. My husband had to close his leather business he had owned for 10 years due to the economy, I lost my contract and lived month to month. Load shedding also became more prevalent. We only have one supplier providing electricity in the country – Eskom. Load shedding is the restriction of electricity use and is implemented by Eskom, to prevent the electricity grid from collapsing countrywide. In a nutshell, you only have one supplier to provide you with electricity and they don't do maintenance or upgrades on the power stations, resulting in them switching off our electricity for a certain period of hours per day.

"The only product in the world asking its clients not to use it."

Each city has its own timetable, which is broken down into subsections, according to where you live. So, if you are in Stage 1, you will not have electricity for two hours a day, but if you are in Stage 4, then you won't have electricity for fours at a time or perhaps twice a day. It is absurd. But this is what corruption does to a country.

I never knew when my last contract would come to an end and that it could end anytime in the economic downturn. We experienced a home invasion, theft of our vehicle, and saw so many of our friends and colleagues being murdered, raped, and tortured for a few earthly possessions.

Life is most certainly hard in South Africa. Over 30% of the population (of an estimated 60 million) are unemployed and half of the 70% left over, are simply living hand to mouth, which means, you work today to earn R50 which will buy you just enough food to feed your family for the day. If you do not work tomorrow, you will not earn that R50, and your family will starve. It is that simple, and that hard.

For those of you who do not remember, South Africans had a vicious system in the 80's called Apartheid. It was a law that prohibited black people from living in the same neighbourhood as white people, and as an added insult, black people had to walk around with a passport when they entered white areas, to prove they were legally able to walk around in the street. Everything was separated. The toilets, the busses, the beaches, and the neighbourhoods. Black and white people were not allowed to have relationships, it was a crime. It was a travesty that stained our country for over 20 years until it was finally abolished in 1993 when Nelson Mandela became the first African president. Since then, South Africa has been run by the ANC government.

I was in boarding school in Springbok when the news broke. They enforced that people of colour had to be integrated into white schools as well as boarding schools. It was a crazy time. Remember, hate is learned. No child is born hating another person just because of their skin colour. In Springbok, there were mostly white farmers and well established old, white-owned businesses. The only people of colour were the helpers on the farms and those doing menial work in the town.

They were deemed unequal to white people. Black people were feared and made out to be monsters who were only there to kill the white people. It was even said that they are not human, for the oppressors to not feel as much guilt when they tortured and killed them. It was sick. That is what fear does to you.

You fear the unknown. Just because of the colour of their skin, they were deemed dangerous. It is still a universal law globally – don't stand out, don't be different, fit in, and be just like everyone else.

If you dare to stand out and be different, you will be ostracised and shunned from the world. Our interconnectedness fights so awfully hard to conform, to belong, to be accepted, that we will do anything to fit in – even if we know in our hearts that what we are doing is wrong.

So, in 1994, my boarding school in Springbok opened its doors to any non- white person who dared to join the school. When I say dare, I mean, have the crazy guts and courage to stand out and be different – and stand out they did. I remember standing in the queue to go into the school hall one day and a farmer's boy, van Rein van Rein (yes, his surname was also his name) stood about 10 meters behind a black boy. He refused to stand any closer. I cannot remember what happened to him, but I think his parents removed him from the school just so that he did not have to be on equal footing to the people of colour. Hate. This is how much hate there was. In boarding school, it was the worst. They shared living quarters, the same showers, and toilets, and of course the dining room. The white boys would all bang their tin cups on the table chanting "nigger lover nigger lover...". This was aimed at the head boy who dared to share a table with the African students. He was punched and beaten, ostracized, and hated just because he dared to stand out and do the right thing. He dared to be different and to protect the African kids from the white hatred.

Hate. It burns so brightly and feverishly that you are left with so little.

I cannot remember the head boy's name, but he was my hero. I used to romanticize him, for being so brave, for standing up against the white supremacy when he did not need to.
Courage, it fills your heart to the brim and makes you want to burst with love and pride.
You see, I am blessed because my father was not a racist, so I was not brought up to believe that African people were evil or dirty or stupid. My father was kind and wise and stood up for what he believed in. My mother's father was a real Afrikaner though, and he hated Africans. I remember watching The Bill Cosby Show once with my sister and he stormed into the lounge and switched off the TV as we were not allowed to watch "stupid monkeys" on tv. My father and him (my grandfather) would have many bouts of heated arguments about race.

Hate. It brings out the ignorant in us.
Those years were turbulent and lit with fear of the unknown and change. People hate change.

The government soon created the Truth and Reconciliation Committee (TRC) that was chaired by the Archbishop Desmond Tutu. For three years the atrocities of the past were heard in the TRC court and people in charge of killing hundreds of African people under the Apartheid law were acquitted and forgiven if they repented and asked for forgiveness. It was a beautiful initiative that had its merits, but three years cannot wash the country clean of the blood that was spilt. I think it should have continued for at least ten years. It is a raw and bleeding wound that has still not healed. It has been twenty-seven years since apartheid ended and it is far from being forgotten. People need a safe environment where they can express their pain, fear, hate, sorrow, and doubts. This committee was a good platform where ordinary folks had the chance to voice their fears.

You see, all we as humans ultimately want is to be heard. We just want to express our opinions and to know that our feelings matter, that you have heard what we said and acknowledge it. We do not always want a solution; we just want to be heard.

It is that simple. Remember that the next time you fight with your spouse or colleague or child. Nine out of ten times, they simply want to be acknowledged and to feel that you will take their feelings and opinions into consideration, whether you do or not, is not the issue.

In the early 2000s, South Africa created a system to try and uplift African people and create more equality amongst them, it was called Broad-Based Black Economic Empowerment - BBBEE.

It meant that companies were encouraged to work with black-owned businesses and employ people of colour in management positions or they would not be able to do as much business with government entities. It is a very clever system they designed to help give previously disadvantaged businesses a chance to get experience and new business opportunities. To put them on an equal footing with the historically advanced white-owned businesses. If a company's turnover is over R5-million a year, they can earn points for either doing business with a black-owned company, training up their in-house African employees, hiring an African employee in management, using and training up an African supplier, and also for donating to a charity. My publishing and events company initially took a knock when this system came into full effect. I would struggle to get the tenders that I was qualified for, and due to my BBBEE level, I would be passed over.

Initially, I rebelled against it and would blame everyone for my business not doing well. But then the true African spirit in me rose again and I saw an opportunity in the challenge presented to me. So, I created a "Your Money Novice Entrepreneur" competition. That was the name of my company, 'Your Money'. I received government and corporate funding to visit disadvantaged schools and teach them about Entrepreneurship and encourage them to attend our one-day workshop where they could learn how to start their businesses and even win the competition on the day. It was hugely successful.

On the same day, we also invited companies to exhibit their products and services and make the day free for anyone to attend. I loved it! I loved visiting the schools, colleges and youth hubs in the townships and northern areas and seeing how their faces would shine with eagerness to learn. My goodness were they hungry for information. I think it was also a case of broadening their minds, to allow them to dream and to think that they too can have their own businesses one day. You must understand, most of the people in the townships live hand to mouth. Most of them have not left the township never mind the city they live in. Their parents are poor, their friends are poor, their grandparents were poor, and everything and everyone around them has very limited means to live. Dreaming is not encouraged. What is the point of having dreams if you can barely feed yourself for a day?

That was the biggest turning point I saw when I spoke to them, to tell them that they too can have a successful business. I encouraged them to think about what they are good at, be it doing their friend's hair or nails, fixing cars, or making beautiful furniture out of nothing. It was about planting seeds, to allow them the luxury of dreaming, to allow them to think that they too can change their own lives. Poverty is but a mindset and they can lift themselves out of it. It was my biggest honour doing this and seeing how they came alive. I know it might sound contradictory, but you can literally start any business in South Africa, with no start-up capital and no need for a qualification, and still make a success of it. That is the true African spirit - we require so little, just a sprinkle of hope, a little push in the right direction, and a truckload of faith, and voila, you have a business.

Clair, a dear friend of mine who grew up in South Africa and the Netherlands in equal parts always said,

"Doing business in South Africa is like the wild west."

Anything goes, and anyone can make it if they have the will. It is exciting and challenging, but anything is possible. I can now see the lure that the wild of South Africa must have held over the Dutch and the English when they arrived in the 1600s.

I tried to find some information on my family tree but could not find too much. Someone once showed me a book where it was written that one of the Erasmus immigrants from the Netherlands married a local Khoisan princess called Petronella. She was the black sheep of her family and an alcoholic and embarrassed her family to such an extent

that they disowned her. Mmh, my big butt and our family's rebellious streak seems to make more sense now...
My father's mother (the first Gwendolynn) leans toward the Irish side. My mother's side was from the French Huguenots and my mother's father, from the English turned Afrikaans' side.
Thus - I am a proper representation of the global village all in one go.

DAY 2: ATTRIBUTES

Make a list of all the positive attributes and skills you have.

Example: Pretty eyes, good communication skills, large network, creative mind, and loyal friends.
Nothing is too small or insignificant to write down. Even if you think everyone knows it or can do it, write it down. You will be amazed by how few people possess what you think is normal or average.

Add one thing you are grateful for. Close your eyes and feel the joy!

Positive affirmation: "I am divinely inspired".

CHAPTER TWO
CROSSING BORDERS

Fast forward thirty-nine years and twenty-one days, and we have arrived here today. We did the near impossible. I am still in a state of shock as I review my life.

It is 4:32 pm, the sun is shining behind scattered clouds and you can hear the siren of an ambulance in the distance.

"Squeak, squeak, squeak, squeak," is all I hear as the kids jump on the bed. My fingers run across the keyboard; my face crumpled into a serious frown as I try to gather my thoughts, "Be quiet". What I would not do for these kids. Over the past twelve months, we fought with numerous lawyers, immigrated from South Africa to the Netherlands under a cloud of secrecy, then five months later packed up everything again and moved to Scotland. To make matters worse (or better, I have not established yet) this happened right amid the outbreak of Covid-19. As I am sitting here, I feel exhausted, stunned, and exhilarated. One minute my heart is overflowing with gratitude and the next minute I am in disbelief. Did we really make it? We just came off a fifteen-hour journey via the ferry, where we had to fight to convince the ferry and border control that we legally have the right to enter the UK. For three intense hours, they held us for questioning to check out our facts.

Under European law, the kids and I could enter and live in the UK legally if we are accompanied by a British citizen. The catch was that the ferry we had travelled on, legally had the right to deny us passage without proper documentation. My face was drawn, my intestines where longing for a cigarette and all we could do was sit and wait and pray that they would agree. At that very moment, all we had was each other, our faith, and a belief that we have a right to a better life.

I kept repeating, "All is well, they assured me everything is working out as it should be. Have faith. All is well, they assured me everything is working out as it should be."

After three painstakingly long hours, the customs official phoned and said he was going to do us a big favour and give our family permission to board the ferry and enter the UK. Good God, I almost cried. It was the best ferry ride we ever experienced. We skipped, jumped, and danced and had there been space, I would have done backflips. We did the most momentous 'Titanic pose' at the hull of the ship and slept like the dead that night.

The following morning, in an old, heavily overloaded car, we drove to Edinburgh. We tried to fit in as much of our belongings as possible, and for the rest of our sentimental and valuable items, we hired five-cubic space to transport here – it should arrive next week, I hope. But quite frankly, I am not too bothered.

Ok, so how did we end up here?

DAY 3: VALUES & VIRTUES

What are your values and virtues? When last have you sat down and evaluated your values and virtues? Have they changed as you aged, and are they still valid? Benjamin Franklin, (Founding Father of the USA, author, politician, and entrepreneur) had a 13-week plan to achieve "moral perfection". He devoted a specific virtue he wished to achieve and focused on that each week.

For example, Week 1: Temperance, Week 2: Moderation, Week 3: Patience and so on. His reasoning was that if he could practice one thing every day for a week, several times a year then eventually it would become a habit, which he would only need to do once every other year and so forth.

Make a list of the values you think you already possess and then make another list of those you still wish to possess.

An easy way to remember the difference between values and virtues is - value is the goal and virtue is the way to reach it.

Example: My Values: Authentic, Adventurous, Brave, Creative, determined, and Curios.

I would like to possess more: Compassion, Generosity, Kindness, Wisdom.

Add one thing you are grateful for. Close your eyes and feel the joy.

Positive affirmation: "I am pure positive energy. I am determined. I am successful."

CHAPTER THREE
QUEST TO IMPROVE

I have been wanting to write this book for almost three years. I have attempted a few blogs, but I just could not bring myself to go any further than that. I do not think I would ever have finished this book, had it not been for the angels' instruction. I have been meditating and praying for so long to become a better person. It is hard to be a good person. I just want to be selfish and care only for myself and my immediate family's needs, but then that nagging little voice inside of me always says, "You are better than this". "No", I would shout out, "I am not better than this. I do not want to be kind and helpful and make other people's lives better or easier. I want to mope and sit on my throne of self-righteousness and point my knobby finger at everyone and yell - look at you and look at you. But oh, please God, just don't look at me and point a finger back at me.

I do not like what I see. My ego is large and likes to get what it wants". I feel like I have been through the diamond cutting machine and have been skived, cut, chipped at, and buffed, and then spat on, wiped down, and the whole process starts all over again. And guess what, I am still not shiny, nor the biggest, brightest diamond in the shop. But I am here, sparkling now and again when the light shines exactly right and hits me at just the right angle. Then oh dear, I sparkle, and shimmer with radiance.

Every single day, I try again and again, and hopefully one day, I can look back at the past few years and say, "Wow, you have actually become a better person. Imagine that!".

With this book, I am laying myself bare for the world to see, and if you can take a lesson or two away from it, then great. If not, then my children will have a little memoir of their crazy moms' life. You see, I also used to be part of the rat race. I think once you are in it you can barely see any way out. We wake up, shower, get dressed, race to get the kids to school, drink our two to four cups of coffee, and then straight into our first meeting we go. By 10 pm we have not even had a chance to sit still for one minute and reflect on our day or the life ahead of us. Before we know it, ten years have passed, and the kids are grown up and do not want to spend time with us anymore (after years of nagging us to play with them and us being too busy). Now, ten years later, we are still stuck in our shitty jobs that we must endure to pay our enormous bills every month. The kids are done asking for playtime, your family have stopped inviting you for dinner as you never had time to join them, and your spouse rarely confides in you anymore. You are not the same person you were, and neither is your environment. You are discontent with life, but you push through as you have a faint belief that things will get better, perhaps at the end of the year, life will become more balanced. But that day never comes. Or more realistically, you simply do not know how to turn down the speedometer.

If it were not for my break-down, the threat of divorce, and nearly being institutionalized, I would probably still be in this race.

DAY 4:
WHAT PEOPLE THINK?

How do you think people perceive you? Write down all the things that you think people think of you.
I like to think that people think I am friendly and funny, but I also think I can be perceived as vain and loud.

Why should you list these? Because I want you to see how it makes you feel when you think of other's opinions about you. I pray that you do not write something ugly about yourself. Try to be kind. I want you to close your eyes and see how these thoughts make you feel?
Why does their opinion of you matter so much?
Will it affect your income or the way you live your life? Probably not. Now take a deep breath in and exhale. Relax and embrace the fact that you are different and unique and not for everyone. Your life will not end if people have negative thoughts about you. It does not matter what they think of you. All that matters, is that YOU like yourself.

Add one thing you are grateful for. Close your eyes and feel the joy.

Positive affirmation: "I am perfect in every way."

Now go out there and enjoy your wonderful, quirky uniqueness!

CHAPTER FOUR
THE STORM BEFORE
THE CALM

I have this theory that things always become terrible before they get better. It appears I must nearly die before my life changes. I once heard someone call it the, "Divine Storm".

You know when you strive so hard towards your goal and then, just when you had enough, and you are about to give up – the break-through occurs. That is why the experts always say: "Never give up," because it is in those final few hours/days or weeks that the break-through is slowly starting to come alive. Just hang in there.

My first heartfelt prayer that I can remember was when I was six-years old, begging God for my father to divorce my stepmother. This prayer became my continuous chant for nine years before my wish was finally granted. It was the happiest day of my life when I heard the news.

My next big prayer was to go overseas and travel the world when I was twenty-years old. I was waitressing at a restaurant, earning a lot of money in the industry for my age, when I decided to leave. A lot of my friends were doing it and I wanted to join in on the fun. Within eighteen months, I had saved up enough money to buy flight tickets, apply for my visas, and have some extra cash to live in the UK for a month.

My third and probably biggest prayer, was when I prayed for acceptance. Isn't it difficult to accept the things that happen to us? I am most definitely a control freak and used to love being in control of just about everything in my life. I sometimes could not breathe if things were out of my control. I have since learned to just trust and let go. After my recent adventure, I now know that God is in charge and he will always have my back.

The Serenity Prayer God grant me the serenity
to accept the things, I cannot change.
courage to change the things I can. and
wisdom to know the difference.

I was two months pregnant with James, and his father, Gerard, did not want to commit to getting back together with me again. We had just been through a nasty break-up two weeks before I found out I was pregnant. I was a second-year student at the time, and had two jobs, to cover my fees, rent, food, and so on. I did not know how I was going to do it all on my own. I was so hurt and of course, angry. I remember driving to my dad's house, laying on his couch, crying and praying. After I said the serenity prayer a strange calmness came over me and I started writing in my diary. I asked God to send me someone who would love James and I and accept us just the way we were.

A mere three weeks later, I met my beautiful husband-to-be, Paul. He accepted us as we were, no questions asked, and just poured so much love over us.

Next was my prayer for a successful business. I started my community newspaper, 'Your Money' in 2010, with no experience in starting or running a business. I was in well over my head. I had just finished my studies and we had a one-year old boy to care for. Paul had also just started a business, so we were both very tight with money and time. Good heavens, I remember sitting up till midnight working on proposals and finishing my paper, and then having to get up at 3 am to check on our boy and then at 6 am he was up again and wanting attention. Within two years, both our businesses started making profits; I won three awards and did the near-impossible in that period by organizing a mini 'Amazing Race' style event in my region - The Incredible Race – Eastern Cape.

I only had six months to put this entire event together. I lost 30 kg and became a walking zombie. I would sometimes wake up and find myself standing at the door or Paul would wake me up saying I was speaking to him or just staring at him for hours. A little psychotic right? But I pulled it off and gained the attention of the people I needed to, to do future business dealings with.

After I closed that business, I worked for an organisation I absolutely adored, but after a while, my desire for my own business peaked again. I was so miserable; I knew it was time to leave. I had asked God for three times my current income and the freedom to do what I love and what I am good at. One day, I became so angry with Him, I shouted, "Why do you hate me so much? How could you allow me to change my life, and wake me up to my potential, but then deny me my wishes? It is clearly all a lie. I do not create my reality, shit just happens!"

I did not meditate for nearly a week, but when I finally calmed down, meek apologies came, and I gently began to flow with my intention setting again. Within a few weeks, my wish was granted, I was earning three times my current salary and I had two big contracts doing what I love.

After our home invasion, I wanted to immigrate to the Netherlands with my family, but for legal reasons I cannot mention, one problem after the other kept arising. It was a year of pure hell, fighting one legal battle after the other and eventually, my husband had to leave us to start the processes.

In September that year, I discovered that what we were fighting about all year – was null and void and in fact – unnecessary. I consulted with my lawyer and I was told that we are free to leave. As easy as that. This made me realize how difficult we always make our own lives. And then we moved to Scotland. I phoned my friend asking if she knew of any jobs in the UK and she said, "Yes", so, I phoned the UK Immigration department for advice. They said I could apply to enter via the Surinder Singh route and I just could not believe how easy it was. According to European law, any family member of a British citizen can enter the UK with their Residence Card granted by the host country – i.e. the Netherlands (for us). I had my card, but the kids were still in process, and we were told that due to Brexit, we had to start the application processes all over again if we wished to stay. I was livid. We were expressly told and reassured time and again, "As long as you apply before Brexit, you will be granted Residency". Well, that did not go according to plan then did it?

Once I made peace with my worst fears, they could not haunt me anymore. I saw them for what they were, just my imagination, and instead, changed my imagination to make it more fun and adventurous rather than playing out the worst-case scenarios in my mind.

> "When you change the way you look at things, the things you look at change," Dr Wayne Dyer.

As you can see, all things considered, my life has been blessed, and I am sharing my life lessons with you in the hopes that you may find hope from my experiences. I believe in my heart that you too can have anything your heart desires. All you need to do is ask, believe that you are worthy of receiving, and then accept the blessings that come into your life.

And of course – now and again – break those damn rules!

DAY 5:
WHAT MAKES YOU
SPECIAL?

Today is going to be a great day. Do you know why?
Because today you will find out what people really think of you, and I know you will be pleasantly surprised. We tend to think and expect the worst when this is in fact, far from the truth.
Send your friends and family a message as follows:
"Hi family, I am doing a survey and would like your honest opinion, please. What do you really think of me? What do you think makes me unique and special?"
Write their feedback down. I hope you frame these beautiful messages and keep them close by. We all need motivation and inspiration during trying times and these uplifting words will see you through many a rainy day.
P.S. If the responses are all negative then: 1. you need to get yourself a new circle of friends, or 2. you need to work on your people skills.

Add one thing you are grateful for. Close your eyes and feel the joy.

Positive affirmation: "I am deeply loved and appreciated."

CHAPTER FIVE
SUICIDE (1980 – 1985)

Trust, such a little word, for such a big emotion. I lost trust many decades ago. Do you remember when you were little and your parents said,
"Jump, I will catch you?"
And then you jumped without doubting for a second that they would catch you. As you become older, you start losing trust in people and yourself.
You doubt everything and everyone because people tell you to. You are told to be afraid of this or you cannot do that, "Don't run, you might trip and fall, or don't sing so loud, people will think you are strange, sit properly, good girls don't get angry," and so it goes. Before you know it, you stopped trying to do what makes your heart sing, and instead, you did what everyone else is doing, just so that you won't stand out in the crowd. So, I stopped trusting from a tender age and taught myself how to suppress my emotions and appear untouched. It was ingrained in me to not feel sorry for myself, and that no-one was going to come and save me, so I had to become self-reliant from a young age. Suppressing my emotions rarely helped me. Instead, it only made me more emotional and fury and anger replaced fear and sadness. I was a ticking time bomb waiting to explode.
I was five years old when my mother committed suicide. We were staying in Vanderbijlpark, in South Africa, after she and my father got divorced. My mother Lea's parents lived close by so they could help look after my sister and I while she was working. I have a few memories of my mother. Standing there as a small white-haired girl outside a petrol station, fumbling with her hands and looking on nervously as her mother drove off in the dead of the night. Her heart was thumping inside her little body, running after the car, with her short and stubby feet, waving, and crying, "Stop, come back for me!"
It turned out that my mother was simply checking if the car was working before picking us up again. We used to lie on my mother's bed

and play with her glass eye while she read us a bedtime story. She was soft-spoken and laughed a lot. She found humour in small things. Once, my mother was bathing me and discovered paint all over my little body. "How did you get paint all over your body?" she asked. Only to discover that while she was at work, all the children were playing a game called "doctor, doctor". Google it if you do not know what the game is.

My last memory of my mother was praying before bedtime, thanking God for my grandparents and for keeping them all safe. Then the next day, she was gone.

We were told that our mother was killed in a car accident. It was not until her cremation that my sister peeled off the cotton wool from the side of our mother's head and showed me the hole from the gun wound. She had killed herself. All that I can recall from the service was that I was feeling very sleepy. That was it. I just fell asleep on my father's lap and wanted to go home. We then returned to live with my father in Port Elizabeth. We loved our father dearly; he is a good man and the best father any child could have asked for. I adored him since the moment I can remember and still do. But then, she arrived. My worst nightmare, Rene.

It transpired that my father had an affair with Rene while he was still married to my mother. According to them, my mother was a happy and social person, but also a manic depressive. My father told me that my mother would be depressed for weeks on end, unable to care for us and that is how Rene came onto the scene. She was a bit older than my father, a uniquely beautiful, strong, and charming woman. She would come in and sit with my mother, counselling her, and look after my sister and I. Eventually, Rene and my father fell in love and decided to end their respective marriages and be together. My mother fled with us to Vanderbijlpark, while my father was in the process of gaining custody. It was too much for her and she decided to kill herself rather than live without us.

Growing up with that knowledge was incredibly difficult. As a youngster, I would often think, was I not worth fighting for? Could she not have tried harder for us? How could she just leave us behind like that? Am I not lovable enough? As I went through my teenage years, I masked it behind sarcasm and a 'the devil cares less' attitude. I would act out and try to shock people with my words and actions. I remember re-enacting the Peter Pan scene with Captain Hook – "Don't try to stop me Smee," for my friends at boarding school and end it with a dramatic death and mad laughter. I enjoyed shocking people. Getting a reaction out of them was good enough for me. I enjoyed being perceived as brave and strong, and I played the role perfectly well.

Once I hit my twenties, I started investigating depression and the feeling of wanting to die. I would hound my few friends that struggled with depression and beg them to explain to me what it feels like. I could not comprehend how anyone would want to willingly end their life. This beautiful God-given gift called life. What could be so depressing that you would want to end your life? What is depression?

Stop feeling sorry for yourself I would say. Life is great. You have food, a car, a job, friends, beauty, what is there to be unhappy about? I would drive them crazy at every 'wine-night' and irritate them with the same questions over and over. How I had so many good friends, I do not know. Then in my thirties, I felt the sadness. I would cry and think, "If only you were here for me right now." But strangely enough, I never hated her, and I never truly mourned her as a person and as a mother. I never felt that strong a connection with her as I always had my father's love and affection, and I was so young.

Today, as I write this, I have an intense pang of sadness for her. I sit here and think, I too have done something like her. I also ran away from everything I knew and loved, to give my children a better life and be reunited with their father. I would imagine giving her a phone call to talk about girly things. I try to remember her voice, but I can only see her face. I have the same body shape as her and my sister looks a bit like her too. I sometimes see my son's face resembling hers.

I have no resentment nor hate for her, just deep-seated sadness, and pity. She must have felt so alone. Not only was she betrayed by her friend and confidante, she also lost her husband and was going to lose her two daughters whom she gave birth too, cared for, and loved as much as she could.

I would maybe say this to her,

"Mother, I am sorry. I am sorry I did not mourn you. I wish things were different for you. I love you. You will always be beautiful in my eyes. Thank you for giving me life, I owe you one." I do not know, it sounds a bit silly, but it is something, right?

I remember as a child there was a soap opera on television called "Days of our Lives." In one of the episodes, one of the main character's mother came back to life. I cannot remember what happened to her, but she was never actually dead, and so she returned to her daughter after many years. I would daydream about the day my mother would walk through the door and we would hug and cry with joy and my life would be beautiful again.

But alas, she remained dead. It used to anger me when I heard people speak about suicide, like it was just a simple word you could roll off your tongue and play around with in your mouth and exhale.

"What do you know about the complexities of taking your own life? How dare you use that word." I would stand there and simmer in my self- righteousness.

"It is mine, my word, my badge, I own it. It is mine." Suicide. The Killing of oneself.

The Catholics believed that your soul would be damned if you took your own life and even denied these tormented souls a Christian burial (and we wonder why so many have chosen to not be called Christians anymore).

My husband and I often pondered our innate need and desire to self-destruct. We as humans constantly seek new and innovative ways to hurt and punish our bodies. We don't understand this throbbing urge to hurt ourselves - or those around us if we are unable to inflict pain upon ourselves. I now believe it is because we are not who we are meant to be. This need is our soul/spirit in desperate need to be freed. I believe that our spirit is so big, that it struggles to be contained in these tiny little human suits that we were born in. And through years of conditioning and moulding, we have lost our own truth. We have become prisoners in our minds and became our own worst nightmares – small and insignificant – but at least we fit in.

No one is pointing fingers at us and laughing because we talk funny or dress differently. Oh no, we are perfect little humans, with the perfect house and our perfectly applied masks to hide our truth – because that is what has been ingrained in us. Fit in or be shunned from society. And that is what I think causes suicide. Our soul's need to be free. The urge to live our truth and to say,

"To hell with you for not thinking I'm worthy enough. I am enough. I am more than enough. I am free, I am beautiful and oh so powerful, and if I cannot have that freedom in this lifetime, then I shall have it in the next."

I have a personal favour to ask you. If you have ever contemplated suicide, why don't you try, to break those damn rules and let your true beauty shine through instead? To hell with the doubters and the naysayers and those living in their perfect little glass houses judging you.

Their opinion of you is none of your business. Break free from your self-imposed prison and shine that little light of yours. We are all connected and born from the Universal Consciousness where we are all meant to love and be loved, to thrive and be joyous! Do not be enslaved to your worst fears, most of the time, it is just an illusion. You are so beautiful and nothing you could have ever done or said will take away God's love for you. You were created in perfection, and you can have and be anything you choose to be, so choose life! Even if it is only till tomorrow. You never know what tomorrow might just bring you. Just one more day, ok? Big hug, x

DAY 6: WHAT MAKES YOU TICK?

What do you dislike about other people?
Today we will do some shadow work. You must be able to acknowledge and laugh these things off and thank them as they are your teacher. I know you do not think it is funny right now but work with me, please. It gets easier and smoother as we go. The things I dislike most about other people are selfishness and being rude. And guess what, I can be rude and selfish too. I hate this about myself. It makes me angry and ashamed that I am inclined to such base emotions. I sometimes catch myself being rude to a telemarketer or I do not want to do something for my husband because I expect him to give up his time, and he should not ask me for mine. It gets ugly dealing with these emotions, but as I progress, I can catch myself in the beginning rather than at the end of the conversation, and try to make a sharp U-turn, breathe, swallow my nastiness and say something nice instead.

Make a list of things you dislike about others.
Please give it good thought as to why you feel this way. Is it a part of you you dislike? Just breath through the process, you are here to accept yourself and to grow from your new found experience. Not to judge you or others. Be kind.

Add one thing you are grateful for. Close your eyes and feel the joy.

Positive affirmation: "I forgive myself and others. I am free."

CHAPTER SIX
STEPMOTHER
(1985 –1993)

But alas, all I had was Rene.

To me, she was a mean-spirited woman. I have never met anyone who had so much anger and bitterness in their heart.

I remember when she moved in with her daughter, Sarah. I was initially so happy. I loved Sarah, she was always so kind and loving towards me. She would play with me and try to make my life more bearable, but at the same time, I had to deal with Rene's bitterness. I later in life came to the belief that she hated me because she had to give up her son during her divorce.

He was about the same age as me and I must have been a reminder for her having to give him up to start a new life with my father and Sarah. I do not know if this is true, as I never had the opportunity to ask her this, but it was a revelation I had a few years ago.

I think it ate her alive every day and I was having to pay for her sins.

I remember how I would wait anxiously for 5 pm every day when my father would get home from work. I would stare out the window and as soon as I heard his car, run outside and straight into his arms. Every day, I would think that would be the day I was going to tell him not to marry Rene, but I was too afraid to say anything in-case she heard and punished me.

The abuse started small. In the beginning, she would just shout at me, smack me on the bum or not give me food.

But it was the way she did it. I am not sure if she told me not to tell my father or if she just implied that I would be punished if I told him and that he would not believe me anyway, but I never told him until I was an adult. In front of my father and others, Rene was a doting mother, but she was as sly, beautiful, and charming as a fox. A mere six months after my mother died, my father and Rene got married. No more calling her aunt, I was told to call her mother, which I hated. I did not understand why I needed to call her mother when she had only just moved in and my real mother was dead, but if I did not, I would not get food or anything I asked for until I did. I remember one day when she was angry at me. She was always angry at me, shouting or hitting me. But that day, she had asked me to take the broom that we recently bought back to the shop and exchange it for a mop. Here is a six-year old little girl, in South Africa, walking with a broom and a till slip, to a shop about 3km away, all by herself, to exchange a broom for a mop. Well, of course, I did what I was told to do, and on the way back I was followed by a man and felt so scared that he was going to pick me up, take me to his house and kill me. When I got home, I immediately told my dad and just cried. They had the biggest fight that evening, and I got the brunt of it later.

It must have been the day after they got married, as I remember the strings of balloons and confetti hanging from the balcony's roof when I hanged my dog. He was a small little dog called Dinky, (almost like a Chihuahua).

I do not know why I did it, but I hung him up by his neck from the string attached to the balcony's slates. He was crying and yelping, and I remember thinking "Oh dear, I think I am killing my dog", and I just let him hang while I looked for scissors to use to cut him loose.

Psychologist reason that when women are hurt, they tend to hurt themselves, or what they perceive as an extension of themselves. "Hurt people, hurt people." I was too small to hurt myself, so I hurt my poor little doggie. Luckily, he did not die that day.

We moved to Oranjemund in Namibia a few years later, and one day, I came home from school and Dinky was gone. He would excitedly wait for me at the gate every day to come home from school.

Dinky was my lifeline and Rene had given him away. We looked for him for a week and she told us that he had probably just run away. Years later she told my dad in a fight that she drove to the outskirts of town and left Dinky there. She hated me that much, that she could not bear to see me have a little bit of joy from this dog.

When we moved to Oranjemund, my sisters went to boarding school in Springbok and I was left alone in the house with Rene every day. I was so jealous of them living in a different city and having an amazing life with friends living in the same building. I thought of their boarding school as utopia and I was in hell. It was about two years after we had moved when my father got retrenched from the mines and was offered a job in Johannesburg. He turned the job down and instead started manufacturing his cleaning material, which became rather successful. Unfortunately, this meant that he was often away from home, and for awfully long periods because he had to drive to all the surrounding towns to sell his materials.

During this time, I contracted jaundice (yellow fever) and was not allowed to go to school. My father was on the road and Rene decided, to hell with it, she was not looking after me. So, she left me some food, told me to look after myself and left me alone for nearly a week until my father came home.

Oh, God, I remember that evening so clearly. I was trembling with fear as I called my sister in boarding school. That is all I knew, that crawling feeling of electricity running up and down my body, that familiar feeling of dread and fear. My body would turn ice cold and then the sinking feeling and dread in the pit of my stomach, heart racing, and nausea creeping up on me. Fear. I knew it so well. Shortly after this incident, they sent me to boarding school too, and life became instantly better. I know beyond all doubt that if it were not for my strong faith and trust in God and Jesus, that I would not have made it this far. I believe that this faith saved me throughout my childhood. Jesus was my anchor. I loved reading the Bible and seeing the difficult things he had to endure and thinking, "Yes, I am also a special child of God, I must suffer too to save the people around me". I was a good kid, with a pure heart.

Soon thereafter we moved into our holiday home in McDougall's Bay. It was such a beautiful place; we had a huge home overlooking the ocean. It was a steep climb down and just two streets further we were on the beach. None of the streets were paved and there was still an old windmill as you entered the village. I loved McDougall's Bay; it was like being on a permanent holiday. This is where I met my best friend Belinda.

After all these years, we are still so close.

We were incredibly naughty back then, but we did not hurt people. Belinda was amazing; she was passionate, loud, and beautiful. She was also English in a very Afrikaans little village, so she did not have that many friends, except for the boys, all the boys loved Belinda.

She helped me come out of my shell and would always tell me how beautiful and kind I was. As a child, I felt very ugly, fat, and boring. I had large, dark freckles covering my entire face and body, I had copper-brown hair which was always cut in a 'pisspot' style.

Rene never allowed me to grow my hair, she said my hair was too thin and needed to be cut. So, I grew up looking like Annie - red, curly, short hair and covered in freckles. On top of that, I had big thighs. Rene nicknamed me thunder thighs or gun-bags.

Growing up I was very self-conscious, I never felt pretty or "cool", but I had the best of friends and they made my life beautiful. We could

41

walk by ourselves on the beach, even at night-time. It was safe for us to walk to town by ourselves, even though the town was 5km from where we lived.

Any child the same age was a friend, and we did not have to ask permission to play, we just joined them. We made up games and used our imagination. Our Barbies represented us and our friends, unicorns and dinosaurs were real and there were no rules. This was imagination land. We even played games with bones. If we were to see a wild horse in nature, we would rally up our friends and chase it to get a chance to ride it. I remember catching and riding my first horse then. I think she was rather old, as she was not fast enough to outrun us, so I caught up with her, jumped on board, and rode her bareback, hanging onto her mane as the reins. I was thrown off a couple of times, got a couple of scratches and the worst that happened was that your friends would laugh at you for falling off. The beach was my favourite hangout place. Mc Dougall's Bay was surrounded by rocky beaches, and I lived on those rocks. I wonder if I even owned a pair of shoes, I should ask my father. I would spend most of my time climbing the rocks and trying to catch little fish with my hands in the rock pools. My father was good at catching crayfish. We would often come home and upon smelling the seafood, exclaim, "Not crayfish again!"

Yes, we complained about eating crayfish and seafood. There it was your staple food; you could survive just on the loot from the sea.

I always knew there were Beings that I could not see or touch, but I just knew they were there. I loved the biblical story of Abraham sacrificing his son. I think it was the martyr in me. I decided that I also wanted to build an altar and sacrifice something, so I made a beautiful little altar on the rocks and offered them a sweet and some flowers and shells. Now you need to know that a sweet, for me, was like gold. Over December we would each receive one packet of sweets and that packet needed to last you the whole month. So that sweet offering was a huge sacrifice for me.

I prayed fervently for all the people in the world, and love and happiness for all. I remember that feeling as I smelled the fresh sea air filling my nostrils and the gentle breeze caressing my skin. As I looked up, I felt like I was flying. The excitement was bubbling up inside of me and I knew they were there with me at that moment, hugging and kissing me. Life was sweet and I was as happy as anyone could be under the circumstances.

Most of the time, not all the time.

My sister Sarah was my lifeline. I truly adored her. She was beautiful, kind, and funny, and everyone loved her. She doted on me and gave me all the love I craved from a mother. She would often intervene when

Rene got too rough with me and would try and calm Rene down or distract her to take her fury off from me. She often succeeded, but most of the time she was just told to mind her own business. I remember the one afternoon I did not do what Rene had asked me to do quickly enough, and she called me into the kitchen. Sarah's friends was standing there and Rene asked me why I did not do what she had asked me to do. I was a bit cheeky in my response because I felt brave seeing as there were other people in the room. I believed she would not hit me in front of them, but what she did was even worse.

I was about twelve years old, hormonal, and feeling self-conscious in front of Sarah's friends. I just remember her face went red with anger, and she started shouting at me, "If I tell you to do something, you do it. You do not ask questions; you just do it. If I tell you to pee in that pot plant, then you do it. Go pee in that pot plant now!".

That familiar fear came crawling all over me again, I could not believe she was going to make me do such a horrible thing in front of everyone. I just stared at her and hoped she would change her mind, but she did not. She had her familiar imposing posture bearing down on me and shouted,

"Do it!". As I was about to do it; she burst out laughing and said, "You see, that is how you discipline a child. Get out of here".

I felt such deep shame burning inside of me for nearly doing what she had asked me to do in front of everyone. I remember the look of shock on their faces as they realized Rene was serious, and that I was going to do it. She had humiliated me to my core. I felt like a street dog. Low, without any self-respect and unworthy. That was her skill, she knew how to humiliate me.

I think she was crazy in pain, love, and lust; I do not know. I think she had more pain than she could bear, and her only outlet was hurting me. I think it was cathartic for her to release her pain.

I could sometimes see the heat glazing over her eyes when she hurt me. It was almost like she had taken ecstasy. I could see the enjoyment, sheer hate, and release when she beat me, and then afterwards, she would be sweet to me and give me a hug saying I needed to stop enticing her to hurt me. She would say, "If only you would listen to me, Lynn. You make me do this to you." And yet I still loved her.

I would always seek her approval and love. I thought, if only I tried harder to be better, kinder, smarter, funnier, and prettier, maybe she would love me. Everything I did was to get her approval and love, it was madness I know, but I could not stop trying.

You see, Rene was a beautiful woman. She was charming and funny, and people loved her. She was smart, brave, and independent, and I wanted to be just like her. I saw how she could love. She adored her daughter, Sarah, and she would get everything she wanted, no questions asked. She adored my father too and doted on him when they were not fighting.

I would do anything for attention, I craved it so much. There was this horrible old man; the grandfather of one of my childhood friends, that would always try to touch us on our private parts. He was a stinky and dirty old man, and always sat on the stoep (porch), so we had to pass him to get in and out of the house. He tried it a couple of times, but I did not take kindly to him and told him not to touch me. I told the parents and they simply told me to mind the old mind and ignore him.

Ok, fine I will ignore the stinky dirty old man if he keeps his filthy, clawing hands off me. I later learned that their daughter, my friend, committed suicide. I do not know why, who knows why a person does what they do, but I always remembered that filthy fucker, sitting on the stoep, drinking from sunrise till sunset.

The one aspect of being sexually abused is that some women receive enjoyment from it, and this causes them a lot of deep-seated shame. "How can I feel enjoyment from someone using my body against my consent for their enjoyment and think it is wrong. I must have asked for it. This must be something I also wanted". And so, for some, they start to believe that they deserve to be abused and perhaps even think it is a form of love. It is such a complex situation. I would strongly advise anyone that has experienced something like this to seek counselling. You need to get help and speak about it. It is never your fault and you did not ask for it! It is not your fault – because you were flirting, or too friendly or wearing a short skirt or low-cut top or whatever the hell these assholes told you.

It is the predator's fault only and not yours! Claim back your power. Remember that you are only a victim if you think you are. You are a powerful child of God and will be truly unstoppable if you accept this fact. No one can ever make you feel inferior or unworthy. How you think of yourself is how people will treat you, so if you think you are not worthy, chances are that is what others will believe too. You are such a powerful being, claim back your innate power burning so brightly inside of you. I pray that one day you will see and understand what I mean by this so you can never unlove yourself again.

DAY 7: WHO ARE YOU?

Today we are going to look at who you really are.
Being a mother, wife, daughter boss etc is important, but it does
not define you. You are so much more than just the labels everyone
(yourself included) places upon you. I used to think that my work made
me who I was and defined me. It took a long time to rid myself of such
limiting self- beliefs. I had to dig deep and think, what defines me?
Do I even need to be defined or can I just make it up as I go?
Today I know that I am pure positive energy, here on earth to enjoy this
beautiful gift and make the most of it. I am spirit and soul; I am love
divine. Some days I am a mother and carer, other days. I am a goddess
and demanding. My partner does not define me, neither does my
background, my parents, my job or even my sex.
So who are you?

Add one thing you are grateful for. Close your eyes and feel the joy.

Positive affirmation: "I am not defined by my job, sex, race or status. I
am pure love and energy."

CHAPTER SEVEN
FORGIVENESS
(1994)

Have you noticed how you miraculously simply endure a bad time in your life? You get up in the morning, brush your teeth, get dressed, and do your work, regardless of how sad, hurt, or angry you are, and this can continue for years on end. Your body can endure so much strain and batter, you can beat it endlessly. You can put harmful chemicals into your body, yet, you endure. Until you break the cycle. We are made to endure. Like iron in a fire, you either bend and become crooked, or come out a beautiful, strong, and shiny sword, able to defend yourself and make something out of yourself.

Have you ever been in a bad situation where you managed to break away from your bad habits or abuser and then you experience the relief?

Normally the relief is short-lived and is closely followed by a wave of searing anger and despair. Sometimes, it is a mixture of anger, despair, and relief, all at once. The worst is when you crave it. You tell yourself all sorts of lies as to why you need the drugs or why they hurt you, this must be our need to self-destruct or for self-punishment, I don't know, but it's insane and some of us will do this to ourselves over and over again until one day, there are no days left. The mind is our most precious commodity. You heard the story about the twins who deal with pain differently. It is how they think about the situation. One will think, poor me, and the other will think, it did not kill me, so it must have made me stronger. You see, torture and suffering can change even the best and strongest among us. It can take our beautiful, pure hearts and strangle them so much that it is difficult to see any love. Anger becomes easier to bear than pain, and while I know a lot of people say anger is bad, personally, it saved me. If I did not turn to anger, I would have turned only to despair, and perhaps ended up like my mother. I often look at my sweet little daughter and think that this is how I was. Gentle, loving and kind, and only able to see the good in everyone. I am still incredibly naïve, and rather choose to believe that people are good (they cannot all be bad) and hopefully one day they will prove it to us. But I have a hard edge to me, which doesn't seem to go away. (I'm striving for life-time achiever award for trying the hardest to become a better version of myself.)

Anger comes from deep-seated pain and suffering that is not resolved. In my case, anger saved me and made me stronger. I taught myself to love less and not feel so intensely. I taught myself that sadness was weak and that I had to be strong to survive. So, I became angry. Once I had finally broken free from my oppressor's clutches, I felt absolute exhilarating freedom. It tasted like candy and power to me and I got drunk on it.

They would call me 'Fireball Express' at school because I had a short temper. I had learned from experience, that people feared angry people. I made a promise to myself that I was never going to fear anyone again, so I showed everyone how angry I was, and the result was that people left me alone. I was never bullied at school, but at the same time, I never bullied anyone either. Instead, I would fight the bullies, as I knew what it felt like to be bullied by someone bigger and stronger than you.

I knew I was strange but did not mind it. I was always a mix of two worlds. A nerd, reading non-stop whenever I had the chance, but at the same time, also the first one to sneak a cigarette when the opportunity arose. I would sing the loudest and pray the most in church, but then around the corner just behind the building, I would be kissing the boys and having a drink when offered.

I was most definitely not what you call black or white, I was all colours of the rainbow mixed.

I loved boarding school. I shared a room with Belinda and two other girls and felt like I had died and gone to heaven because I could spend every minute of my life with my friends. Can you imagine the happiness I felt? I made so many friends from all over. It was like being a bar of chocolate in the chocolate factory and getting to hang out with all sorts of different chocolates, all the time. If I felt like some nutty chocolate, I could hook up with my crazy friends. If I felt like debating serious topics, I could call on my neurotic friends, and if I just felt like having some fun, I could call on Belinda.

In boarding school, you wake up when the bell rings, get dressed, make your bed, and then the bell rings again to signal that it is time to eat in the joint dining room. Once you are finished eating, you go back to your room, pack your school bags, and when the bell rings again, you leave and walk to school. We stayed just across the road from school, so it was a three- minute walk.

I think you learn a lot about people at boarding school, and I know I became more tolerant of people that were different from me and learnt to appreciate their uniqueness, instead of seeing it as a hindrance. If you wanted to go to a friend's house for the weekend, your parents had to send you a signed letter to let you out. I was rarely allowed out, so I spent most of my weekends there. I loved that too though, I loved pretty much everything about my new life.

Nine years later, my father came to visit us from boarding school one day and told us the news, that Rene and he were going to get a divorce. I was ecstatic, my God! The instant freedom I felt that very minute, pure elation, and joy. I was going to be free from her at last. Source had finally granted me my wish. It only took nine years.

At the end of that year, my father, my sister, our dog Butch, and I, packed our bags into our bakkie (small utility truck) and off we went, back to Port Elizabeth. It was a two-day drive. I cannot begin to describe how light I felt. Here I was for the first time since I could remember, free from the woman I perceived as evil, my oppressor, who had been hurting me for so long. No more! I felt like a new person, perhaps better described as someone who was in a torture chamber for nine years now suddenly, released. The world looked completely different to me.

I saw everything with fresh, new eyes, just like a baby. I stayed with my aunt Lee and my sister stayed with my aunt Mary, as their respective children were closer to our ages.

I remember the shock when I arrived to hear my cousins call their mother by their name, sometimes in jest. The first time I heard it, I thought my aunt was going to release hell upon them, but she just answered their question and carried on with what she was doing as if nothing had happened. I could not believe my eyes. I then heard my eldest cousin swear in front of his mother and she once again just carried on with what she was doing and said something like, "Don't swear" and nothing more.

No beatings, no shouting, no abuse.

I started going out to clubs with my other cousin when I was fourteen years old. Suddenly, I had all this freedom to do as I pleased, with no one shouting, hitting, or restricting me. In hindsight, it was way too much freedom for a girl of my age who had previously lived a very sheltered life. My father did what he could and raised us as best he could, I think he just wanted us to be happy. He realized the trauma I had experienced under Rene's reign and so he thought he was doing me a favour by giving me all that freedom. I, of course, used it to the maximum. By that time, I was smoking as much as I wanted to with his consent, and I went out to clubs with my older cousins. I was drinking way more than my body could handle and yes, kissed way too many boys, but I never had sex with them. That much I kept for myself. For me that was special, and I did not want to just give it away to any random person.

I was nineteen years old when I lost my virginity to my first serious boyfriend. He was a kind boy and adored me. He was loving and gentle and respected me. I am proud of the fact that I was the oldest and last one in our group of friends to have sex. For me, it was not a light matter and I felt that having sex with someone, was like giving a piece of myself to that person. I started to value myself; I knew I was different, but I was ok with it. For once, I embraced my uniqueness, and I was ok standing apart from the others. I did not mind being different, strange, or crazy, as that was who I was, and I loved it.

When I was eighteen years old, I moved to Cape Town to stay with my sister for a bit. While I was there, one day, Rene came to surprise us, and it was only me that was home. I have never felt so uncomfortable. She was being friendly and loving and I just sat there frozen. The familiar fear crept over me again, and I had to remind myself to just breathe. Then, Sarah invited us to go down for a weekend and visit her. Rene lived just down the road from her. We went, and that evening we went to a bar. I had so much wine in me that I plucked up the courage to confront Rene. We sat around the corner, drinking our wine, and talked about the past. I asked her why she hated me so much when I was little, and how she could treat me like that. She just cried and said she did not mean it like that and that she loved me, but I was a difficult child. She said I would constantly question her, asking so many questions, never happy with a simple answer. She told me that my mother was not a depressive, that she was a very lively and happy person and that she loved us so much.

She said, "I am sorry for hurting you. I did not know how to handle you". That was a huge turning point in my life. I felt like an ignorant farm girl who had slain a dragon with only a stone. In hindsight, it turned me into quite a ruthless person. I felt untouchable, like there was nothing I could not do or have. I felt invincible and immensely powerful. I had made my tormentor cry, with mere words as my weapon. For many years to come, that power was too strong for me, and I ruined many relationships as I believed I was untouchable and that everyone should be grateful to have me in their lives. My ego was inflated to the point of bursting. At the same time, I will not deny that I became an overachiever since then. When I went back to Port Elizabeth (from Cape Town), I studied PR and Journalism at Damelin College. I walked away with the Cum Laude award and excelled in everything I did. I had achieved everything I wanted, but there was still a hard edge to me. I was unforgiving and fearless, and there was nothing I was afraid of.

I remember driving my African friend home on New Year's Eve. She lived in the centre of the city and the street she was staying in was where all the local clubs were. There must have been 10 000 people gathering that evening and partying in the streets. I could barely see straight, but I was driving my Beetle like it was a sports car. We stopped in the middle of the street as we could not get any further. We were stuck for nearly an hour, until eventually I got out of the car (the only white person in sight) and started shouting at everyone ahead of us to move their cars so I could get through. It was a sight to behold. My poor friend kept trying to pull me back into the car, but I was high on adrenaline and the alcohol had started to wear off. Believe it or not, the cars eventually moved for me to get through.

I can't mention my Beetle without sharing some funny stories about my history with these cars. My first car I received was when I was eighteen years old, a gift from my dad. It was a gold station wagon and within in the first week of ownership I crashed it. I wanted to race a random person in a beautiful red Polo, yes dear reader, with my old 1980s wagon. Needless to say, it didn't go well, and I took out one of the oldest cement blocks on the corner of Summerstrand and asked my sober friend to say he was the driver... (I never claimed to be nice.) My dad was so angry and told me to pay back the money he spent on the car, which I did and then he bought me a Datsun. Unfortunately, the car was more in the workshop than on the street and then I met the first car- love of my life. She was a beauty. She was metallic silver, an original 1970 Volkswagen Beetle classic and my sister gifted her to me. My heart still makes summersaults when I think of her, I loved her so much. She was a quick fix, nimble on the road and easy to jump-start. And she had this huge, original steeling wheel and all the antic buttons and gadgets intact. Did I mention I was in love?
She could drive 1500 km, easy peasy lemon squeezy and go straight to 35km per hour in second gear. On a rainy day, you can push-start her and within a few seconds she would start.
She had the honour of having the international comedian, Barry Hilton push-starting her one night after being stuck.
Oh, and my poor, dear friend, Sally. I stayed with her for a while and I drove us home after work one night. I warned her to keep her hand on

the door as it didn't close properly and I took a sharp corner wildly, (I never did drive her except wildly and with brimming excitement.) I'm still jabbering and the next minute I look to my left and the door was hanging wide open and no Sally sitting next to me. She fell out of the car as I turned the corner.

Oh, my goodness, she was so angry with me. She had to get stitches and could not work for a week.

We would go away for weekends and just park at the beach, make a bonfire and then when it gets too cold, go cuddle up inside my sweet Beetle and sleep there for the night.

Beetle almost never had breaks. When we drive down a hill, I would immediately start pumping my breaks and try timing it to perfection so that I don't have to stop dead at a traffic light. But if I see that I am not going to make it by the time I get to the bottom, then I would start pulling up the break handle. You would spot me a mile away. You would just see this flash of silver speeding past you, but five seconds later, you would pass me as I crawl towards the traffic light in the hope of it turning green before having to stop. There was never a dull moment with Beetle around. My friends would make bets before they step foot inside Beetle,

"Chances of survival one, two or four." Well they didn't die did they, so we couldn't have been all that bad.

So, I liked to think of myself as an adventurer, but it was more like arrogant. Not so much in my later (more mature years), but certainly for most of my twenties and thirties. I was arrogant and simply unstoppable. I learned a lot about this from Rene. She taught me to be strong, to be confident and fearless, and above all else, to never feel sorry for myself.

I learned from her to always push, and to never accept defeat. I would always push and fight, looking to have my own way, no matter what. Rene kept in touch throughout the years, sending wishes on our birthdays and Christmas. This was probably her way of reaching out and letting us know that she did love us. The thing about memory is that it can be tempered with. You could have been shown a photo, riding a horse when you were young, and your mind would have created a memory folder for it. Ten years down the line, you say, "I remember riding horses when I was young," when in fact, you cannot remember riding it. Your memory, however, recalls that picture and it takes on an entire new memory. I often wonder, how much of my memories are true and how many did I recreate to suit a story at a time. Deep down, beneath all my bravado, I was just a scared, broken little girl who did not feel like she was worth loving.

Abusing alcohol also didn't help, it only masked my inner most turmoil, blurring out most of my beautiful God-given gift called life, all because I did not feel worthy.

About two years ago, I travelled a fair distance to see a spiritual counsellor. I could not stop hating Gerald and I thought I needed to heal from this emotion. During our rather intense session, I realized that I was there rather to heal from Rene. I realized that she could not help herself. I felt that she was in so much pain from leaving her son behind, that she did not know how to cope with it.

The card I drawn was the 'Ghost Dance', which said that I needed to cut the chords with karma.

Situations; where I feel helpless and vulnerable, would keep on appearing if I did not sever the chord with karma now, and forgive her. I cried so hard, my entire body was shaking as I let out the screams of terror, fear, resentment, and longing for her love. But that night I said farewell to her in my mind and forgave her for everything she has done. I then realized that Gerald and people like them, would keep on entering my life, until I truly see them for who they are, children of God.

I needed to accept and forgive them and move on.

About a month ago, I was making myself a cup of coffee and looking for a new tin of condensed milk. I was getting a bit edgy as I now only drink condensed milk in my coffee – and then it hit me.

I used to get so annoyed making Rene millions of cups of teas and coffees and always with a spoonful of condensed milk in it. She had a glass jar filled with condensed milk that only she could use – (even though I would sneak in a spoonful or two every now and again.)

I just burst out laughing and said; "You are having a good laugh up there aren't you Rene. So, I ended up being just like you after all."

In the end, I have learned a lot from this woman. How can I hate her now when I am because of her? How can I resent my mother for what she has done if I am because of her? They taught me to be strong, to be resilient, to be joyous and brave in the face of adversity.

They taught me to love with everything I have, to not have any regrets and to live as if today is my last.

And for that, I am eternally grateful for these two strong women who birthed and raised me and showed me – that I am enough after all.

> "There are two great days in a person's life – the day we are
> born and the day we discover why." - William Barclay

DAY 8: TIME TO DREAM.

Today we are going to dream.
Close your eyes and dream up your most beautiful, dreamy life.
What does your perfect life look like? Who is in it? What are
you wearing? Where are you and what do you smell, see, hear,
touch and taste?
Go into as much detail as possible. If you are not smiling while you are
doing this, you are doing it wrong. You should feel giddy and excited
with anticipation. This is the life you have been dreaming of – right
here in your mind's eye.
Dream it, feel it, taste it, know it is yours for the taking. Write
it all down.

Add one thing you are grateful for. Close your eyes and feel the joy.

Positive affirmation: "I can have anything my heart desires. I am
worthy of receiving it."

CHAPTER EIGHT
BEING A TEENAGER
(2020)

My father in law always said that eighteen-year olds should run the world. At first, I laughed, but then I thought back to when I was that age and now, I agree. They have the maturity, from their eighteen years of life experience, to make a few important decisions, but most importantly they are not yet marred with bitterness and hopelessness. The world is still their oyster, anything they can dream, they can achieve. They have passion and excitement and a lot of energy to implement the hard decisions that need to be made. They do not just enjoy talking about things but prefer to take immediate action. I think we can all agree that we need more implementation and action from our politicians, and less talking and conferences to talk even more about how they are planning on finding a solution to our problems. I digress. The reason I am talking about teenagers today is because of a talent show I watched in the Netherlands. It was put together by twelve to fifteen-year olds from a local school. Please do not laugh, but it moved me to tears. There I was sitting in the front row, with tears streaming down my face as these youngsters belted out, "It's just a like a movie", by Adele. So why was I crying? You see, what I saw on stage that night, as these beautiful young souls were baring their essence, their hopes, and dreams for all to see. It was so raw, so brave, it took my breath away. I felt so little in front of them and I realised how much I had changed over the years. I could see their awkwardness on stage, as they were trying to pronounce the English words (it was a Dutch school) and at the same time, they were trying not to look foolish in front of the audience. What made it even more spectacular was that in the front row, there was a group of boys of about thirteen-years old, laughing at the girls on stage, but the girls did not stop performing. They did not run off the stage and hide. Instead they braved it like little soldiers and finished their songs with their shaky little voices and the look of uncertainty glinting in their eyes. I was in awe of these youngsters performing on stage, it really made me re-look my life and it was not so nice. I remember being their age, feeling awkward, and in love with a boy, and wondering if he liked me too. I remember not knowing what my body could do and how each body part felt separate from the rest of my body. It all felt out of proportion. My eyes felt like they popped out and my gums stuck out too much when I laughed. I hated how my thighs jiggled when I walked and how my dress flopped around my big bum. My arms felt too long, and my head felt too big. Nothing felt like it fitted right and on top of that, as a woman, you have your monthly period and your emotions run all over the show. Such intense emotions, it was like my body was on fire. The one minute I would be bent over in pain from the stomach cramps, and the next minute I would be trying to walk like a supermodel when my crush was in sight.

My hormones were all over the place. I loved boys with such intensity and then I hated them with the same ferocity when I saw them kissing another girl. My world would collapse, and life felt like it was not worth living anymore. Then, a month later, another boy would attract my attention and the hope would well up again. And so, it went on and on for most of my life. I think why I felt so sad that night was that I missed how quickly I was able to bounce back from failure and disappointment. Within a few days, or worst-case scenario, a month, and I was back on my feet and deeply in love with another boy again. I missed my endless positivity and how hopeful I was. I honestly believed that the universe was there just for me.

I felt special and knew that there was something important I had to do. I did not know what it was, I just knew I was meant for greatness. It was not a case of being big-headed, it was just a simple fact that I knew in my heart to be true. I have not felt that special in an awfully long time. My hopes and dreams were sucked out of me and I often felt like a major failure.

That night I cried for that optimistic, fiery, happy, and energetic young girl that I was. The girl who dreamt that anything was possible, that I was the master of the ship, and I could have and do anything I wanted. The girl who experienced a disappointment and just shrugged it off and tried again. I cried for that girl with her big dreams and aspirations. The girl who went through so much, baring herself to the world, only to be loved and accepted, who has been hurt and bent and became so crooked that I do not recognize her inside of myself anymore! Where is she? She must surely still be inside of me? How do I release her, how do I win her over and prove to her that she was right, that you can have anything your heart desires and the world is your oyster and you are the master of your ship? I want her back and I want her to sing for me with her shaky voice and I want her to shyly look at what she wants and put on her performance clothes and go get it! I want her to walk like a supermodel spotting her dream life. I want her not to care about the laughing boys in the front row and close her eyes and dance like no one is watching. I want her back and I want to love her and reassure her and make sure she never hides from me and life again. The following weekend I did a beautiful letting go ceremony and set my new intentions for the life I wished for. I wrote the following:

I want to be so happy and excited about my new life that I have butterflies in my stomach from pure joy.

I want to let go of the past and only think about the present moment. I want to live with positive intentions.

I want to recapture my sense of wonder and awe in all things that are created and be grateful for the beauty in its simplicity.

I want to experience my abundant energy, positivity, joy, and love for all – as when I was a young girl. I want to have that carefree, 'the world is my oyster' attitude again.

I want us to look forward to each day and appreciate the splendour and freedom that comes with this wonderful gift.

I want to explore new countries, travel extensively, be more adventurous and do something new or learn a new skill each term.

The power of intention setting. I wrote this in February 2020 and a mere three months later they all came true. What are your intentions for your life? How do you want your life to be? Write it down, imagine it, believe it to be true and so it shall be. Surrender and Release. And for heaven's sake

- break those damn rules you set for yourself!

DAY 9: THE DARKNESS

What is the darkness inside of you? Are you ashamed of her?
What are you most ashamed of? Is it something you did or something someone did to you?
Write down the experience and breath through it.
Let the emotion wash over you as you remind yourself that you are only human. Mistakes are made. Forgive yourself or that person and breath.
Please do not stay in this emotion for too long. Be aware of the feeling it creates in your body and accept it.
For a long time, I was ashamed of the things I had done when I was inebriated. It was hard to look up and face them, but I did.
I saw them for what they were, forgave myself and moved on. My mistakes do not define me, it simply means I am human.
There is no wrong or right answer.
Be gentle with yourself, there is no need to berate yourself over and over for what happened.
Make peace with it, apologise if you did wrong and move on.
You can only become a better version of yourself if you keep on trying.

Add one thing you are grateful for. Close your eyes and feel the joy.

Positive affirmation: "My past does not define me."

CHAPTER NINE
TAKING A GAP YEAR
(2004 - 2006)

I remember the excitement of going to the United Kingdom for two years. It was a wonderful opportunity to see the world and meet people from all over the world. I saved up enough money to get my visa and had enough cash to sustain me for a month. I do not think my dad knew this, but when I boarded my flight that evening, I had no idea where I was going to stay. I arrived at Heathrow Airport at 6 am. It was March 2004. A twenty-four- year-old girl from South Africa, with a head full of dreams, a huge backpack on her back, a smaller bag in the front, and another bag in one hand. I was strong, I was eager, and I had no idea where I was. I searched for the TNT magazine at the airport shop; it listed all the different rooms available to share, per suburb. I spent the next two hours going through the list, phoning from a telephone box, and finally decided on one room. I bought a map of London and off I went on the tube, "Please Mind the Gap."

I cannot remember the suburb I was looking for, but it was a vicious two- hour walk to the place. I arrived to meet a sullen girl, wanting me to pay her share of the rent for the month ahead. I could not fathom paying that much money upfront and not dealing directly with the owner, so off I went to the phonebook again and found a room to rent in a house in Leytonstone. The owner was very friendly and gave me good directions to the train station. Upon arrival at the train station, he met me and walked me to the house.

I did not move for about a week after that, I was knackered. I shared the house with eleven other people from all over the world, Poland, South Africa, England, Italy, and Australia. My roommate was an Australian girl, and we instantly disliked each other but, when you are that young, you simply do not care where you sleep as long as it resembles something soft underneath your body with a blanket on top.

I loved London. I had such a good time meeting up with all my South African friends that were already there and my beautiful British friend. I struggled to find the perfect job, (I should rather say, I struggled to find a job I thought I was good enough for), so I ended up working at a cafe inside a business complex. I was not happy there, so I left and ended up running out of money very quickly.

Eventually, I decided that London was not for me and found a live-in position in a tiny village called Eden, just outside of Banbury, Oxfordshire. So, I packed my bags once again and went off to Waterloo station to catch my bus to Banbury. I remember being so sweaty and tired by the time I reached my bus; I accidentally went to the wrong station.

I cannot remember exactly but I think I was at Waterloo East instead of Waterloo Station. I just remember half running after my bus as it was about to take off. I showed my ticket and got on.

The bus ride was supposed to be two and a half hours, so when the time came and they had not announced Banbury, I just assumed the bus was running behind schedule. I mean this happens in South Africa all the time, right? Well, this is the United Kingdom and busses do not run behind schedule. When the bus conductor stopped at 10 pm that night and said, last stop, my heart just sank. I said to him, "But sir, my bus was supposed to have stopped at Banbury Station!?".

Well, guess where we were? We were at Salisbury, home of the famous Stonehenge! Do not get me wrong, I always wanted to visit the beautiful Stonehenge and feel the magic of the stones, but not at 10 pm with £5 to my name.

The conductor was not very sympathetic and said there was nothing he could do, and I should have changed at Heathrow Airport to get onto a new bus that was going straight to Banbury. I am not going to lie; I was a bit scared. I had no idea where I was, it was a Sunday evening, everything looked closed and I barely had cash on me. I remember asking the conductor if I could sleep on the bus until the next day so I could find my way to the right destination, but he looked at me as if I was mad, said no and walked off.

I looked around and saw a phonebooth and phoned the lady who I was going to work for. She answered the phone in alarm and said she had been waiting at the bus station right up until an hour before and had no idea what had happened to me. I explained my situation to her, and she took down the number of the phone booth I was phoning from and said she would phone me back in 5 minutes. It was the longest five minutes ever.

Eventually, she phoned back and said there was a Youth Hostel in the area who would open their doors for me. She offered to pay for my stay and booked me a new bus ticket for the next day. Relief tastes sweet! So, off I went again, walking up the dark street, only the crickets for company when I heard a loud bang and laughter around the corner. I quickly went to see what was going on and to my amazement, I realised that it was the bar being shut down for the night and the last bit of scoundrels were being chased home. Two young boys, probably about eighteen years old were walking towards me with their arms around each other's necks as they sang and managed to keep their feet in front of each other.

I said, "Hi, sorry to bother you. May I ask for your help please? I am looking for the Youth Hostel, I am a bit lost and not sure how to get there". "Of course, lassie, let us walk you there", they said, and poof, they grabbed my bags and off we went up one hell of a steep hill to reach the Youth Hostel just before midnight. I slept like the dead that night and the next day I was back on the bus, but this time I reached my destination.

Sadly, I did not stay long, I think I managed three months there, the village was just too small for me, so I looked for new work again. I remember trying to make friends with the locals, but I would never get invited to a party or anything. One day I had a few too many drinks and I asked my landlord why everyone was avoiding me. He said, "We see so many foreigners come and go, what is the point of trying to make friends if we know they will leave one day."

I felt like he punched me in the face. So, they would rather ignore me and not become close, than to reach out and perhaps make a friend for life – because we will live in different towns or countries. I did, however, meet a lovely Australian guy there and he took me to see The Lord of the Dance theatre show in Cambridge and meet my other hero – Shakespeare's hometown – Stratford-Upon-Avon.

I left and visited my friend in Ireland while I was looking for a new job. I found something in another small village, but this time it was in Scotland, close to Montrose. Here I met some lovely people and one of the girls who I became friends with is still one of my friends today. I met and fell in love with a local man, but he later went to jail and broke my heart. I even went to visit him in jail a couple of times, but as you know the saying goes, 'time heals all wounds'. After the heartache, I moved on once again to another village. This one was pure magic. While I stayed in Edzell I saved up some money to go on a tour through Scotland's scenic places and one of the places we stopped at was Dunkeld. It took my breath away. I remember praying under the beautiful lush Royal Fir trees, overlooking the River Tay and the 16th century half restored Catholic Church behind me, saying how wonderful it would be to live here. And then just like magic, one year later, I did.

#Manifestation 101

I was looking online for new work and googled 'Jobs Dunkeld'. They had a waitressing job available at the Hilton Hotel and I immediately applied with a motivational letter, saying that I had seen this place a year ago and fallen in love with it.
"I would be honoured to work at your beautiful hotel and live in Dunkeld", I said, and so, I moved to Dunkeld. I lived in a dormitory with about forty people from all over the world. I shared a room with a gorgeous local lass, she was so sweet and funny, and we got on instantly. I learned a lot about people there. I must admit I was a bit of a snob because I thought I was better than other people, but I learned to be humbler there, to get to know people from all walks of life and to understand them on a deeper level.
One thing I learned was not to look down on people who cannot speak English well. I used to snivel and sneer at people in South Africa if they could not speak English well, whether they were Afrikaans or Xhosa, it did not matter, I looked down on them and thought myself superior to them.
In this dormitory, I met people with degrees behind their names who could barely converse in English with me, and I came to understand that just because you are born in a poor country, does not make you poor or stupid. I never said I was a great person. I most definitely was not the nicest person to be around though. Going overseas was the best thing I could ever have done for myself. I think most people would agree that it changes you for the better. From my travels, I became more understanding and open-minded. To my shame, the only other country I visited was Germany and the reason was one word... Beerfest! In case you missed it, I did love drinking and having a good time, so obviously I had to see the biggest beer festival straight from where it originates – Munich, Germany. It was a jol, the little that I can remember of it. To be honest, I cannot really remember getting off the plane or getting back on it. Did I tell you I speak school German? Well, it was more like a gibberish version of English, Afrikaans, and German, all mixed together and I thought I was the queen of conversations with anyone that looked remotely German. Like the saying goes, 'When in Rome...'

DAY 10: INTUITION

Practice listening to your intuition.
Ask yourself a question, close your eyes and focus on that question. Put one hand on your heart and one hand just below your chest.
See how you react to both yes and no.
The answer that scratches is the wrong one, and the one that fills you with joy, slight excitement, or a serene stillness, that is the one.
If in doubt – leave it out!
Keep doing this until you find the knowingness inside of you. You always know what to do.

Add one thing you are grateful for. Close your eyes and feel the joy.

Positive affirmation: "I always know exactly what to do."

CHAPTER TEN
A MATURE, PREGNANT
& WORKING STUDENT
(2006 – 2008)

After I returned from my two-year working holiday in the UK, I felt lost and without a purpose. I had just tasted a new way of life and I was turning twenty-seven years old, but with no career.

I did a three-month gig as an assistant tour guide for a disabled tour group. It was exciting. I had the honour of touring all the major game farms, Kruger National Park, Sabie Game Reserve, Cape Town, and various other tourism hotspots. I loved it. I was young, fit, and energetic and I enjoyed working with the people and seeing the wild, rapturous nature of my beautiful country.

Just outside of Kruger Park, is a place called Hoedspruit where a special Hippo lives. Her name is Jessica. She was but a new-born calf when the local Joubert couple found her stranded. This was due to a large flood in the year 2000 in Mozambique that affected parts of South Africa. They reared this hippo as if their own and today, you can still find her close to their home in the river-bank where you can feed her a bottle of rooibos tea from a teat, (under strict guidance, of course, hippos can be very dangerous and you should never attempt this on your own). Google her, it is a heart-warming and interesting story.

South Africa truly takes your breath away, and if you ever find yourself in a position to go on a guided tour, do it. It will stay with you for life. Unfortunately, after three months, my drinking became a problem for my boss, and he advised me to get help. So, I was a waitress yet again and wondering what the heck I should do with my life.

I decided that I wanted to study again so I investigated journalism and decided to enrol. I worked double shifts and saved enough money to pay for my first year of studies.

The second year a dear friend of mine offered me a job at the airport where I could work shifts and was still able to go to university in between. I worked from 06:00 – 13:00 or 13:00 –21:00 and went to class before or after my shift.

On weekends, I would do extra waitressing shifts and that was pretty much my life for the first two years of university. And in between all these mad times, I fell pregnant. I had been seeing Gerard on and off for a few months.

Two weeks after our break-up, I found out I was pregnant. I thought perhaps we could try again for the sake of the baby, but luckily, he said no.

I think he knew how badly suited we were. We were remarkably similar, we enjoyed going out, being social and having a good time. But you need balance in a relationship, and we were no match.

He said he would help me look after the baby financially and would like to be part of his life.

I was however shattered. Here I was working two jobs while studying full time and now having to raise a baby on my own. I was filled with such an intense rage, anger, and hate against this man.

My life came to a 360-degree standstill and I had to change everything. My food, my environment, my clothes, my car, my home, but he could just carry on with his life as if nothing happened.

I was an emotional wreck. Obviously when you are pregnant, your body is filled with all these hormones and there is life growing inside of you. It is the strangest, most magical thing to experience. But I was devastated. I could barely look after myself, how was I to bring up a little human into this world? Just a month or so before this, I crashed another car. I knew in my gut that God gave me this baby as a second chance to start life again.

Or at least to stay alive.

I was dealing with abandonment issues again from my mother and I did not know if I could be a good mother. I didn't have the best role models as to what a good mother looks and act like. How am I going to raise a baby by myself? I was scared, I felt cornered and I felt abandoned, thrown aside and shunned.

By God, did I burn with searing anger and a feverish hatred. I really struggled and did not know what to do.

I was about two months pregnant when Gerard and I had another fight. I had asked him to try and work things out with me again for the sake of the baby, but he said he needed to seek guidance from his parents.

At the beginning of the book, you would have read my manifestation testimonial about how I met the love of my life, which I will share in more detail with you.

DAY 11:
NO COMPLAINTS

Today you will not say one negative word or complain.
I want you to get an armband or hair elastic and wear it around your arm all day long.
Every time you complain or say something negative, snap it on your wrist. Do this for the entire day.
Tell your family and friends about it up front and let them help you stay accountable to your actions.
You are going to be shocked how often you catch yourself doing either one of them.
At the end of the day, write down how many times you complained – it is staggering, right?
You should make this a daily habit.

Add one thing you are grateful for. Close your eyes and feel the joy.

Positive affirmation: "My life is perfect just the way it is. I am grateful."

CHAPTER ELEVEN
A LOVE STORY FROM
HEAVEN (2008)

My flatmate and I went out for a glass of wine one evening, yes, I still had an odd glass of wine here and there. While listening to the music, a handsome, strappy young lad came swaggering over to our table. He politely asked if we had met at my place of work before. I explained that I did not think so, but, because I meet so many people, it was possible. He said he had bought a charger from me at the airport one day and he thought I was the most beautiful girl in the world. I was taken aback. The man in front of me was decent, very handsome, funny, intelligent, had muscles from Brussels and was so well-spoken. He met me at the airport, not at the bar, tick, he was funny, tick, we could talk all night, tick and he thought I was the most beautiful girl in the world. Not sexy, but beautiful, tick. I liked this man. Two other things that grabbed my attention was that one, my friend could be a bit abrupt and sometimes rather mean, but he was not scared of her. And two, I am generally not very approachable and do not look inviting enough for someone to just saunter over and talk to me. It rarely happens. I was seriously impressed.

That night we kissed, and he took my number. We started seeing each other over the next few weeks and soon I realised that I was developing strong feelings for him and I could sense that he really liked me. Then I had to break the news...

To this day, it was one of the hardest things I ever had to do. I had to tell this funny, kind, awesomely amazing young man, that I was pregnant with another man's child. Can you imagine the anguish, fear, and trepidation I felt at the thought of telling him? But I had to. So, I invited him over for dinner one night and afterwards, I said, "I have something very important to tell you".

I sat there twiddling my thumbs and looking around nervously, and this carried on for twenty minutes. I could not form the words to speak it out loud, I was unable to say the words. Eventually, I just squeezed my eyes shut and blurted it out. I was shaking and sweating, even though it was autumn.

I was too scared to look at him, I had no idea how he would react, and I was so nervous that he would just walk out, and I would never see him again. I felt like a little child again, helpless, and vulnerable. And then he said, "Is that it? I thought you were going to tell me we are related, my distant cousin or something!".

I swept my head up and just stared at him in disbelief. "Is that it, what do you mean, is that it?"

He just laughed and came over to me, hugged me and said I am the most amazing, brave, and beautiful woman he has ever met. I could not believe my ears. I had just told him my dreaded news and he just laughed it off as if it was nothing. We talked for hours on end and to this day, I have never met anyone more kind, gentle, strong, amazing, funny, and loving than my husband.

Every morning I say a prayer of thanks for my two children, my husband, our health, bodies, minds, and opportunities in life. He is my rock and my foundation, and I shudder to think what my son and I would have become if we did not have him in our lives.

He is so patient with us. I am the fiery, passionate, fly off the handle, get shit done one, and he is the chill on the sofa, set up a plan and see how we can do it over time, one. I hold intense love and gratitude in my heart for this beautiful human being. I know without a doubt that this man is what I was praying for on my father's couch that day.

Years later, I found out that my husband's mother, at forty years old, was about to go for a hysterectomy, when their doctor friend whom they were visiting told her the weekend before her operation, that she was pregnant. My dear darling husband was almost not born.

I believe God kept him for me and our family. Egotistical maybe, but I do not care; he is made for me and me for him – forever. Now just to add an interesting part to the story... This doctor friend of the parents, who saved Paul's life, is from Italy.

Can you guess in which town? A little town named after our girl. We only realised this after we baptised our daughter. Poetic justice much?

DAY 12:
REPEATED PATTERNS

What bad things keep happening to you over and again?
Today we are going to look at all the bad things that keep
happening to you.
This is the important life lesson you need to learn to overcome.
It will keep you stuck in the patterns you find yourself in over and over
until you have learned the lesson.
The one lesson Rene taught me was that hurt people hurt people and it
is not always about me. This statement taught me that I cannot control
other people's actions, words, and feelings. I can only control how I
deal with them. Do I accept the abuse, or do I calmly remove their
clutches and walk away?
This was probably the biggest lesson I learned, and I had so many
people enter my life who created the same response that Rene did
in me. I would feel powerless and vulnerable and end up hating that
person for 'making' me feel this way, but no-one can make you feel
anything unless you allow them to. I had to learn to love myself more
than anyone else possibly could and to understand and truly know how
worthy and powerful I am.
Think about the things that keep on happening to you and write them
down. Try to think why this is happening to you, what important life
lesson do you need to learn here? It is going to take some courage and
stripping yourself of your ego, but you can do this! Just breath through
it. You are enough.

Add one thing you are grateful for. Close your eyes and feel the joy.

Positive affirmation: "I am not bound by Karma or other people. I
choose the life I want and know I am worthy of receiving it."

CHAPTER TWELVE
SOMEONE LIKE YOU
(2008 - 2010)

So back to my studies...

Life became a lot more interesting and happier with Paul in my life. He made everything so much better and lighter.

When I reached my second trimester, I was very tired, running around working two jobs and studying. I would often find myself at the doctors asking for a sick letter as I just needed to sleep in now and again. I was surprisingly healthy and strong; I slept an average of five hours a night, and my baby was growing bigger and stronger every day. I remember after the September holidays, when I returned to university and received my results.

I failed English terribly. I went from getting 65% down to 43%.

One day, I asked to see my teacher, and she flat out told me that university was not for someone like me. I was taken aback.

"What do you mean, someone like me"?

I asked. She said that university was not for older students who are pregnant and working. I just stared at her with fury in my red face and stormed out of her room. I then went to see my senior lecturer and told her the story. I told her that if I failed my year due to her prejudice against me, I would sue them. Needless-to-say, since then, I would without fail, always get 50% or if I was lucky 51% for English.

I knew I was due that October, the same time I had to submit projects and tasks for final marks. I spoke to each of my teachers and told them I would be unavailable from mid-October to the end of October. Most of them were very lenient and helped me get my projects done. I also had a wonderful teammate who worked with me and helped me wherever he could.

On the morning that my water broke, I was due to hand in my politics folder. I scribbled the last bit down on a piece of paper, left it in my post- box, and told my fellow student to please include it in my draft for the project. Paul stayed at my house making everything pretty and clean, while my aunt joined me in the hospital. They induced me twice during that day but still, no James, and at 7 pm, I was finished.

My water had broken at 5 am, I had been in labour for sixteen hours, yet still no baby. I struggle to remember the next three hours as I was in such agony. I think I became delirious and even swore at the nurses. Then, I heard a male voice asking who my doctor was and why he had not been called in any earlier. He was angry.

Just a few weeks before this, we had an assignment for university due. I was sitting in court listening to the proceedings of one doctor suing another doctor for malpractice.

His wife had died under this doctor's supervision, so I was shit scared. I could not believe that my life and the life of my unborn child, was now in this man's hands.

I cried and vomited, and the next minute I was out.

At 21:35 my beautiful, chubby, strange looking but healthy baby boy was born. He was 4.02 kg and 56cm tall, he was huge! James had been struggling to come down because my hips had not opened properly, so he got stuck. His head was shaped like a cone and he had this tiny little orange curl on his head. He was the ugliest baby I ever saw, I cried and asked God to please make him pretty. They cleaned us both up and put us in a private ward. I will never forget that warmth and smell when they lay him down on my chest, good God, it was beautiful.

I remember the weight. He was so heavy and he looked so helpless and all he needed was me. Just my warmth and my milk. I would be enough for him. Just me.

That realisation was so overwhelming. I felt the strongest affinity, love and protectiveness for this little human, this little piece of magic I created in my womb. I could never have imagined love could be so beautiful and pure as when I looked into his beautiful brown eyes. I was lost forever and life would never be the same again. I would never be lonely again. I would never be alone again. For the first time in my life, I experienced true love. I kissed him all over, smearing his precious little face with my salty tears and I squeezed him so tight. I promised him that night, that while I may not be the perfect mother, I would love him, protect him, and give him a joyous life filled with laughter and adventure, no matter what.

I never backed down from that promise.

DAY 13:
SABOTAGE

What are your limiting self-beliefs?
Money does not grow on trees. Rich people are mean. Men are dogs.
Women are selfish.
Today you are going to investigate your beliefs and turn them on
their heads.
You might not know it, but you have many hidden layers of limiting
beliefs tucked away in your subconscious mind.
I only realised that I did not believe I was worthy of receiving goodness
and kindness when I stopped drinking. I remember shortly after I
stopped, I did a soul discovery course with some amazing ladies and
I was crying when I told them how blessed I felt. I was not crying
because I was happy, but because I was confused and felt guilty that
I was not worthy of it. I kept saying, "I don't deserve this, I don't
understand why I am being blessed, I don't deserve joy," and they
said, "But you are worthy. You have done nothing wrong. You deserve
happiness and joy; it is your divine right".
It has been three years since, and I still need to remind myself that I am
worthy of blessings, love, happiness, peace, and prosperity. I have to
say it to myself over and over. It does get easier though.
So think about all the beliefs you hold, write them down and examine
if they are for your highest good? If not, then it is time to release them
and set new believes.
"A belief is just a thought and a thought can be changed." Louise Hay

Add one thing you are grateful for. Close your eyes and feel the joy.

Positive affirmation: "I am worthy of receiving blessings and happiness
in life. I deserve love."

CHAPTER THIRTEEN
THE WORLD NEEDS MORE
ENTREPRENEURS (2008 - 2010)

Fast forward to April 2010, and I had completed my Journalism Degree, graduated, celebrated my first anniversary with my love, my beautiful boy was six-months old and I had just started planning the birth of my next child – Your Money Publishing.

It was a good decade. I had always been intrigued by the idea of starting my own business. I felt the urge but had no idea where or how to start. About eight months after James was born, a friend of Paul's contacted me to ask if I would be interested in starting a financial magazine with someone he knew. I was excited and eager and of course, said yes, so, I met with the man named Tim and we started plotting the existence of 'Your Money'. It was the most exhilarating time of my life.

Good heavens, I loved every second of it. The planning, the research, the trying and failing, and eventually five months later we had a paper. Unfortunately, things did not work out with my partner. I felt like I was doing all the work and he felt that it was his initiative to start the company so we just could not get to grips with it. Eventually, he signed off and I became the sole owner of the company.

I am forever grateful for Tim including me in the venture and I would never have been here if it were not for that break.

I now understand the lure of working for oneself. It can become very addictive. It is the constant rush and hustle to get out there, get your products seen and sold. I am so in love with this hustle, but it can scar you if you ever need to go back to working for a boss. When you run your own business, you make all the decisions by yourself in a short space of time and you need to trust yourself impeccably.

When you work for a boss, they have their own way of doing things and are not always open to new ideas. I am diverting slightly, but one of the most important lessons I have learned over the years is to always be open to new ideas.

I might sound judgmental, but I do not think you should be in a senior management position over sixty years old. Not the CEO or Managing Director or President or Prime Minister.

We are all hardwired into a certain way of thinking due to our past experiences, and that makes it extremely hard for us to accept change the older we get.

You will notice most of the progressive countries are run by people younger than sixty. Almost 90% of the most innovative companies were started by people in their twenties and early thirties. I believe it is because they are open to new ways of thinking and not marred by fear to take a risk. Countries that are run by young leaders tend to be more progressive and innovative. Keep a lookout for the following countries and see what I mean. Finland's youngest Prime Minister, Sanna Marin is thirty-four.

Jacinda Ardern is thirty-nine and New Zealand's Prime Minister. Ukraine's Prime Minister Oleksiy Honcharuk is thirty-five years old, and Nayib Bukele is El Salvador's thirty-eight-year-old President.

I am not going to lie by saying it is easy to start a business.

It is not for the faint-hearted. You need to be resolute; you need to be passionate, a self-starter, you need to have confidence like it is no one's business, and most of all, you have to love what you do.

It is not for everyone.

I know a lot of people that started businesses and hated it. The thing is, you do not have the luxury of knowing that you are going to earn your set salary every month, especially in the beginning. Chances are you will not make much money as most of the profit will have to be ploughed back into the business.

I initially had no income as I had to give this project my undivided attention. I had no idea what I was doing, and I had a one-year old son to care for as well. My husband also started his business at the same time, so he had to put all his attention into his business. Often, I had to borrow large amounts of money from my father or friends and family to just pay the printers, not earning a cent for myself.

Paul carried all the costs of our living expenses.

As I told you before, we moved to seven different places over two years just trying to keep our heads above water. It was rough. We eventually moved to Paul's parents' house to give our son some stability and to allow us to invest our money back into our businesses. We stayed there for over two years.

Now you must remember, I had been living by myself since I was seventeen years old, and now suddenly, I had to live under another person's roof. I was terrible at it. Even though Paul's parents were the most easy-going people, they never interfered with our lives or told us what to do, I was still miserable. I needed my freedom, but at the same time, our businesses were doing so well.

I won three awards over that period, my profit increased by 50% and my husband's business was also exceeding our expectations. I remember my friends thought it was the funniest thing that I was named in the 'Top 40 Under 40' in 2011 as part of the Nelson Mandela Bay Business Chamber's initiative. We were dirt poor and I barely knew what I was doing. But I guess I faked it hard enough to make people believe in me.

A few months later I won the Regional Businesswomen Emerging Entrepreneur of the Year Award and then later that same year I won the Vodacom Journalist of the Year award under the Community Media category. I had also just completed my pilot project, The Incredible Race.

As you might have noticed I was extremely competitive and there was no such thing as NO for me. I just do not seem to comprehend the word; I believe it stands for 'Nudge On' or 'New Opportunity'.

I lost 25kg that year because I could not eat from stress. I was on a Bulgarian diet of coffee and cigarettes. I had a few lapses where I would be sleepwalking or just stare at Paul in the middle of the night. But I pulled it off and made a name for myself.

We finally managed to save up enough money to put down a deposit on a house and bought all our furniture cash. It was an interesting time. Looking back, I would say my success in my business was largely due to being a waitress in my youth. Waitressing is a form of being self-employed, well in South Africa it is, as you do not just get paid to work at a restaurant, sometimes you even have to pay the owner a fee to work there. But all that aside, it can be very lucrative.

I remember being seventeen years old, (I matriculated when I was sixteen), moving out of my parents' home, and renting a flat I shared with my cousin on the beachfront in Port Elizabeth, all because I earned enough money through waitressing to pay for all my expenses. It also paid for my two-year trip to the UK and my studies.

The Art of Waitressing

I believe every youngster should be a waiter or waitress at some point in their lives. It teaches you about life, people, yourself and even running a business.

Know your product or client.

As a waitron, you will be asked numerous times what you have on offer, what the special of the day is, and what you think they will enjoy eating. People love to be told what to do. Most of us live such busy lives, and we have to make 100's of decisions every day, from some as small as what time to get up, what to eat for breakfast, and then lunch and dinner. What to wear, what route to take to work, when to phone someone, and so it goes the entire day, by the time you reach your restaurant, it is such a pleasure to have your meal already taken care of for you. To help you choose a great meal for your client, you need to know exactly what is on the menu, what is good, what is not so tasty, what is healthy, and even what drink you should have with each meal. I learned that if I knew my menu well then, I could put my customer at ease, they would then relax, drink, and eat more and my tips would become bigger. We worked on tips in South Africa and sometimes you could earn up to R3000 in one evening (that is about £150), and in more upmarket, 'posh' areas, especially over the holiday season, the average earning potential was R6000 and over, for a month.

How to deal with people.

This is something I feel great gratitude for. I met so many different people from all walks of life and I don't think I would have come this far if I didn't learn first-hand from a young age how to read and deal with people aka emotional intelligence. I learned that no matter how well dressed your clients are and how expensive their meals and bottles of wine are, the order does not dictate how well they tip you.

I served so many wealthy people and not all of them tipped well or even at all. I used to get excited when I got a table of people who dressed nicely and ordered all the most expensive meals. I would neglect my less wealthy looking tables and pour all my attention into that table. After five hours, when they were ready to leave, their bill was R5000 and they only tipped me the mandatory 10% i.e. I earned R500 for the five hours I spent on them. In the meantime, my couple table who shared a starter, main, dessert, and bottle of wine, tipped me 30% and I barely gave them any attention.

The first restaurant I started working at was Spur on the beachfront in Port Elizabeth. I remember serving this single guy who was sitting in the smoking section and ordering bottomless coffee for most of the morning. He would eventually have a small breakfast just before the 11 am cut off and end up staying until lunchtime.

His bill was a mere R50, but he always left me a R50 tip as well. I found it so fascinating how a guy could spend the same amount he spent on his food on me too. It was the last time I felt irritated to bring him yet another free coffee or the sixth glass of water. From then on, I treated all my clients with the same respect and attention to detail, regardless of their race, age, or how wealthy they seemed, to me. Perceptions are deceiving, trust me on this one.

The ones that look wealthy enjoy spending money on themselves, not you... But then again, you cannot judge.

Boy, did I learn how to sell there! Spur taught me how to read and treat people. I stayed there for two years before I went to work for a Brazilian restaurant and entertainment bar. I had the party of my life there. It was a constant learning experience. We would get training at least once a week, whether it was a new meal, cocktail, or wine, they made sure we knew our products off by heart. The thing about knowing your products is that it gives you the confidence to sell.

You feel more comfortable asking your clients what their needs are. Once you listen to what they have to say, you can confidently make your suggestions and they will feel more relaxed in the knowledge that you know what you are doing and have their needs and desires at heart. If you can learn the skill of listening without interruption, then half your battles are already won. It is then up to you to keep suggesting what else they should try, without sounding pushy, as no one likes a pushy person – ever! It is a skill you learn, how to ask them what they want, make suggestions, take it in, then pair it with drinks, and send it off with a dessert and another drink.

If you mastered the skill of reading people, then you would know if they were the type that wanted value for money or quality over quantity. You must know which one they prefer, as they normally detest the other type. Also remember that you only have them for an hour or two, so use that time wisely. Make sure they leave feeling that they received value for what they had and that they were satisfied and had a great time. People do not get to feel pampered and treated anymore, so take your time with them and make them feel relaxed and let them have a memorable time.

People do not remember what you said, they remember how you made them feel.

This skill will stay with you for life.

Learn how to build your network and reputation. I eventually got offered a job at another restaurant to manage the day team and the kitchen. I loved working there. It was a popular Scottish restaurant and pub in the main area of Port Elizabeth. All the girls were pretty and wore tank tops and short kilts. They were friendly and always had your drink ready for you as you walked through the door. Here I learned to network and build my brand.

You learn a lot about yourself as a waitress.

You need to have confidence, be friendly but not too friendly, be professional but also playful.

You learn how to pitch yourself to different groups. At this restaurant, for some reason, we always had large groups of people coming in at the same time and hanging out in that same group. An average group of people we would serve drinks to all day and night was between five and twenty people. It was rare to have two people sitting together at a table unless they were in the restaurant area eating a meal together. I learned here not to get offended, and this is a big one.

I was most definitely not the prettiest girl with the best legs or biggest boobs, but I was one of the wittiest and funniest ones and I had a great memory.

So, I used what I had and built my groupies based on these few facts. I could keep an interesting conversation, I had strong opinions and I always tried to make them laugh. They always came back on the nights that I was working and only I could serve them. The same went for the other big groups who only wanted the prettiest girl to serve them and they would only come in on the evening that she was working for her to serve them. Whether she already had ten tables as opposed to our two each did not matter. We would not get the table unless she asked them if it was ok and then we had to make sure we put our best foot forward and served them better than before, as they might then just be ok with us serving them the next time.

This is the pub where I told you I made so much money, I was able to pay for my visa to the UK and support myself there for two months, plus still comfortably pay for my costs while working. Do not get me wrong, there was a lot of flirting involved and most of our clients were men who had just finished work and were looking to blow off steam, but it was never sleazy. It was light-hearted and respectful, and we always had to maintain that level of professionalism or our reputation would be ruined.

I am still in contact with the owner of that restaurant and regularly saw my old clients at business meetings. I even got a contract from one of my regular clients that had their own business and wished to advertise in my publication.

When I moved to the Netherlands, one of the girls I had worked with before contacted me out of the blue and we ended up reconnecting our special bond and became great friends again. Another good friend of mine who happens to be the daughter of my then boss offered me a job too and we reconnected as if it was just the other day.

Then another girl I had worked with during this time offered her home to us as an address to use to get our documents in order. It is amazing how people from your past pop up and you simply reconnect with them as if nothing changed. That is the impact we made on each other, so much so that years after we had not seen each other, we still had that connection and trust in each other to do business together.

That is what it means to have a good reputation. Making that connection, I never understood how connected we all truly are.

Looking back over those waitressing years, I realised that our clients mainly came to see us to connect. Yes, they wanted something to drink, but they could do that at home. They came to the pub to connect with another human being.

You see, we are all truly interconnected and it is a natural need and desire to feel connected with another person, to feel like you matter, that someone is listening to you.

I feel sorry for the youth of today as we have become so disconnected from each other through online games, social media, and the level of crime increasing, therefore, we cannot just send our children to go and play outside. We are too worried that someone will abduct them and do horrible things to them, so we have become disconnected. We need to take regular time out to connect with our inner voice and allow ourselves to trust in the universal flow of life. See, understand, and accept how interconnected we are.

I used all these lessons I learned and implemented them in my business. I thrive on a challenge; I loved the excitement of going out there and trying to win people over. It was a game I played well.

I became well connected and enjoyed the privilege of being an expert on youth entrepreneurship. I was interviewed frequently on the radio and TV and was even interviewed on CNN about Financial Literacy in the Eastern Cape. I created strong liaisons with the different media houses, without them perceiving me as a threat but as a colleague. Alas, after eight years, I closed the paper.

The print industry had become old school and the advertisers started using social media and radio, so print was the last resort.

I am not sorry I started or closed the paper; it was the best learning experience, and no university could ever have taught me these lessons. But it was also one of the hardest things I had to do. It became an integral part of my identity.

My events were still profitable, and I kept that going for another few years. Everyone knew me as Lynn from 'Your Money'. I was invited to exclusive events and parties because of my brand and I was asked to do talks at Universities and networking events, sharing tips and advice with them. It was a great honour for me to be so well known and respected for my knowledge. I cried for many nights at the thought of closing the paper and had tried everything.

I even created an app for the paper, but it was too late, it cost me money every month and it was just not worth my time anymore.

A piece of me also closed off when I shut my doors. It was rough on my ego as I believed that people would forget about me.

When I told a dear colleague (who became one of my closest friends to this day) about my fears, she burst out laughing and said, "Bokkie, you are Lynn freaking Erasmus. You are a powerhouse, and nothing can stop you.

Everyone loves you. They are not going to forget you just because you don't have a paper anymore."

My dear sweet, beautiful Claire, she mentored and mothered me during so many trying times.

This is another thing I feel deeply passionate about. When you become involved in the business, it takes over in your life. You find that you perhaps do not have as much to say to your old friends as before because all you want to talk about is business. This happened to me and I became close friends with a couple of work colleagues I had business dealings with. I think it is a natural progression and if done with care, you can make long-lasting friendships.

I find the older you get, you tend to keep to your group, you don't open the doors to new people and before you know it you have only your immediate family around you. Some people like that, but I love having friends and I think it is important to keep you in check. So, maybe the next time you want to close the door on becoming friends with a colleague, just try to open your heart and invite them in. It might become the most beautiful friendship you ever found. We are not meant to be alone. One of my dear mentors once said to me, "To be a successful entrepreneur you must fail a couple of times to succeed". I hated the thought of failing, but in hindsight, it was the best thing I could have done. As the popular saying goes, "It is not how many times you fail but how many times you get up again". Failure teaches you about what you are capable of in life, how you handle the bad and overcome these challenges.

They mould and transform you into a better person.

I have failed at so many different business ventures. I opened and closed my newspaper. I started a training company with a partner, but it did not work out. I started a company that assisted businesses in becoming compliant with the Consumer Protection Act. The partnership fell through due to personal relationships becoming sour. Then I opened the coffee shop which I closed three months later with hundreds of thousands of rand in debt. I then started coaching businesses and offered marketing makeovers, mentoring business owners and providing them with training on becoming culturally intelligent and selling like they are in love. This was successful and I would still be doing it if we had stayed in SA. I am in the process of building my brand here in the UK, so hopefully one day, I can do what I love the most – coach and inspire others to follow their dreams.

In the first chapter, I briefly explained the Broad-Based Black Economic Empowerment (BBBEE) law of South Africa. I loved the intricacies of this system and through my 'Your Money Youth Entrepreneur' competitions I hosted over the years, I had a magnitude of start-up entrepreneurs on my books in need of mentoring and training. One of the services I offered companies was to pay me to train a few black business owners and help them become self-sustainable. I loved every second of it. I still believe I have a role to help people and I found such pleasure in being able to help people just by sharing my knowledge and skills with them.

It is that easy. That is why I love the idea of mentorship. We all need a mentor, and we all need to offer our services to mentor those in need. We are all interconnected remember.

A lot of people asked me if I was embarrassed that I have failed so many times, and I always say, "No, at least I tried and I have learned lessons that will last me years to come, what have you done?"

How will you know if you are good at something if you have not even tried? I think the schooling system is partly to blame for the fear of failure. We are programmed to fit into the system, to get good marks so that we can go to the top universities so that we can get the best jobs. I am sorry to say this, but employment is not going to be the same in 30 years as it is today.

Look how much has changed in the past 10 years alone. Just take Covid-19 for instance. How do you think work is going to change from this angle?

You need to seriously start thinking out of the box and break some DAMN rules!

How to start a business from scratch?

Before you start a business, I would advise you to think about why you want to go this route. Is it because of a burning desire to change the world by introducing your divine product or skill to the market or simply because you think the prestige will be great, i.e. the ego? Become self-aware about your desire to start a business. Is it out of necessity because you cannot find a job, or because you do not like working for a boss or because you honestly think what you offer is superior to anyone else? I would suggest that you research entrepreneurs and understand the hard work that lies ahead of you. You can forget about working 9 am – 5 pm, it is more like 5 am – 11 pm. Forget about that nice salary at the end of each month, for the first few months, if not years, you will be lucky to break even. It is incredibly hard work, but once you get it, you will never turn back.

I think most addicts enjoy being entrepreneurs, it is a rush and high on its own. You do things on your terms and work obsessively on your business because you know what you put in; you will ultimately get out. What need are you going to serve? How are you going to solve their problems? Remember, as much as you like to think being a business owner is the greatest thing, it is pointless if you do not have customers. So again, what problem of theirs are you going to solve? How are you going to solve it? Got it? Now tell everyone. Make a list of the skills and assets you already possess. It can be your ability to sell, to spot a problem before anyone else and instantly know how to solve it, or it can be your network, knowing the right people in the industry you wish to operate in.

It could also be that you have a great quality camera and a passion for taking photos and a small space where you do shoots from.

Then make a list of your weaknesses and the challenges you foresee, and then state how you are going to overcome them. Do a lot of research on your business idea. Look up companies that offer similar products and services to you. Where are they based? What are their prices? And who are their customers?

I must advise a word of caution here though... Do not and I insist, do not obsess over your competitors. It is good to know them and always keep an eye on them, but never become so obsessed with what they are doing that you lose focus on what you are doing.

List your products and services and give a clear description of each. Work out the pricing.

The cost of your product will be the cost of the raw materials, the energy used (water and electricity), the rent you have to pay (if you cannot work from home), the cost of marketing your product and then your mark-up or profit you need to make on each product. If it is a service that you deliver, work out your hourly rate.

Do not sell yourself short. Know your worth from the beginning, but do not be greedy and out price yourself in the market. This area is going to change constantly in the beginning as you find hidden costs or ways to make your product or service cheaper etc. If you are not good in this area, then find someone that is.

Another important part of running a successful business is to surround yourself with the best team. You may perhaps be good at creating the product, but a poor marketer, so make sure you get the best marketing manager to get out there and market your products. If you cannot hire someone just yet, search for a template on the internet and create your own comprehensive marketing plan. This will help you ascertain who your clients are, where they live, why they would want to buy your product and how are you going to get the product to them.

How does your market feel about you or your product?

You also need to learn to network like a pro. You need to get out and meet people, find out what they like, what they are talking about, and where the world is going. Be part of the conversation and part of the change. You will meet a lot of likeminded people as well as those that will challenge you.

You must learn how to communicate. This is a big one.

You need to be able to communicate your thoughts and ideas to your client, staff, stakeholders etc in a clear and concise manner. What you think is logical might not be to the person you are communicating it to. Also, I am not sure if you noticed, but no one can read your mind, so tell people what you think, what you are doing and what the processes are. Where are you in the production of the product? How long will it take? Some people do not enjoy speaking on the phone, but it is necessary to cut out any misunderstandings. I learned this perhaps a little too late in the game, but always send a follow-up email after an important meeting or telephonic discussion to reiterate what was discussed and the plan going forward. Ask them to confirm receipt of the e-mail to safeguard you. Miscommunications are one of the many reasons for the failure of many businesses that had success written in the stars.

If you want to have a dry run to see what a potentially difficult customer will be like, pitch your business to your family. They are honest and will spot every single little hole in your plan and make sure you know it. Please wear your protective armour before you go in, pitch your idea, take notes, and get out, and then go and have a bath to wash off all the negativity. Try not to take it to heart, just remember the constructive advice you received, fix the areas that need fixing and keep marching on. You've got this!

Remember your why.

Why did you start a business? It is also crucial to enjoy what you are doing. If you are having fun in your business, you will never work a day in your life again. Passion is equally important and cannot be learned. A positive, can-do attitude will take you places that no degree ever will. Life is too short to do something you hate. Learn to trust your gut. Go out there and believe in yourself and your product or service and it will all flow. Learn to listen to that little voice that scratches at you when you need to make an important decision.

I was offered a 50% partnership in an up and coming lifestyle magazine, but something just did not feel right. Later that week, I was speaking to one of my customers, when they mentioned this person. I shared my experience and he just said, "Do not do it!".

The man was painting the town red with lies, making promises that he had no intention of fulfilling and was hoping to use me as the face of the company to get the magazine off the ground. My customer said, "I have seen how hard you have worked to get where you are, you cannot destroy that with one negative association".

So, I thanked the shareholder, and we went our separate, merry ways. You will quickly learn what your Unique Selling Point is. Something that sets you apart from everyone else. This does not mean it should be 'my price is cheaper'. Very few people only care about your price, it is more about the feeling your product or service invokes in them. I had the privilege of coaching just over one-hundred-and-fifty different business owners, managers, and employees while I was contracted to work for The Business Chamber. This one question was always the pivotal point.

Many times, I would have people bursting into tears when we got to this point because they either did not know what made them special or they had forgotten. They had forgotten why they started the business, their passion and drive. There is not one person on this planet, that does not have something special about them. What makes you special? Give it some thought. This is where your story comes in. What is your story? Where do you come from? Why did you decide to open this business? What excites you? Why do you choose to do this if you can do something else?

Be willing to make yourself vulnerable and share what makes you tick and what excites you. People buy from people and they are ultimately going to choose you based on the way you made them feel. It is that simple. How do you make people feel?

Get a mentor. If you want to take your game to the next level, get yourself a mentor that will guide and mentor you through your next stage. My big breakthrough came early in my career while I was working part-time for an Afrikaans newspaper house. They asked me to cover a story about The Businesswomen Association which obviously piqued my interest, so I joined them.

They had the most amazing mentorship programme that changed my life 360-degrees. I cannot stress the importance of being mentored enough. It is like having your own coach in your business, giving you pointers, advising you, connecting you, and guiding you.

Remember the golden rule to pass on your good fortunes to others.

Once you have reached the level of success you wished to achieve, then it is your duty to pass it on and mentor the next person. Remember, we are all connected. In South Africa, we call it Ubuntu which is a beautiful Xhosa word that means, "I am because we are." If you help those around you, eventually it comes back to you too. I used to love taking on interns. I always had one or two interns (at one point nine) working with me. They are so impressionable and hungry to learn; all they seek is guidance and someone to shine a light on their journey. Be that light.

I always say, at some point in your business, you will enter the warzone. You need to be on the lookout for potential threats and opportunities for your business. Get your battle plan ready. What is your strategy? What do you want to achieve? Success? Fame? Riches? Legacy?

What are your plans to achieve this?

What resources do you have (skills, knowledge, contacts, staff, computer, savings)?

Who is the enemy (bad planning)? Who needs saving (customer)?

Now go out there and conquer! Set SMART goals. Your goals must be specific, measurable, achievable, relevant and time bound. Be focused and stay positive.

Speak positive words into your business. Never say, "I am failing", or "I am terrible", or "I am useless".

Use only positive affirmations and soon that is what you will see all around you.

Be authentic. There is no one in the world like you. You are unique, so use this to your advantage.

You know that sneaky feeling you get when someone speaks and you think to yourself, "This person is bull-shitting me!".

There is absolutely no way you would know this for a fact, but your bullshit alarm just goes, "Liar".

We just seem to know when people are lying to us and when they are trying to take us for a ride. Do not bullshit. Tell the truth, be your authentic self and people will be drawn to you naturally.

Be kind in your dealings. In this harsh world, kindness is the most precious commodity you can find, and life has a funny way of coming back to you and dishing back what you did to others.

It does not cost you anything to be kind to your staff, suppliers, customers, and yourself.

Please respond to e-mails too, it is plain rude not to. I do not care how busy you are, if someone connected with you and you invited them to send you an email, then have the courtesy to respond and be honest. You know you are not going to buy from that person, and you do not have the heart or the time to tell them, but please do. Just say, "Thank you but I will not be buying from you right now. Let us see again in three months time." That saves you from feeling bad ignoring all future emails from that person and you save that person the anguish and their time to focus on new customers.

Treat your staff the way you would treat your customer.

Your staff is not only the face of your business but also an extension of your company.

Remember, there is no person who will spread rumours quicker than your staff members (your brand), so you decide what that rumour is going to look like. Happy staff, successful company, satisfied customer, positive bank account.

And now, my secret little ingredient. It is a 100% safe proof path to success. Are you ready? Can you feel the excitement bubbling up inside of you? Great! Now visualise your success.

I am not making fun of you. This is very serious and the most important ingredient to success. You must be able to visualise your success.

You can use it anywhere, anytime. You don't need experience, skill or money to use this and it guarantees your success. So how does it work? Close your eyes and see the name of your business on a building. See yourself happy and smiling next to your nameboard, while you are holding a huge check with £1 million written on it. Feel the excitement and pride of seeing your successful business coming alive in front of your eyes.

You only need to do this for one to two minutes a day. You can even use it before an important meeting.

Visualise yourself sitting in front of that person and go through the motions of what you are going to say to him or her. What is it that you want, how is it going to work, why are they going to love your proposal? See the joy on their faces as they see the benefits of working with you and then you shake hands and signing the contract.

Just a little word of caution here. It must be for the greater good for all. It cannot be done if it is only for your benefit. It has to be for the greater good for all parties concerned. You can even use this method to have that very important conversation with your lover, friend or family member.

Use this visualisation method just before you have an important conversation with them and see the magic come alive. I absolutely love utilising this power of intentional creation. So can you.

The power of branding

I wanted to list branding above, but I felt it needed an entire chapter dedicated to it. I love branding, it is so much fun. Maybe it is just me, but it really makes all the difference in your business.
Let us start with the basics. What is branding?
"Branding is the process involved in creating a unique name and image for a product in the consumers' mind, mainly through advertising campaigns with a consistent theme. Branding aims to establish a significant and differentiated presence in the market that attracts and retains loyal customers." – The Business Directory.
This describes it in theory, but in practice, "Your brand is what people say about you when you are not in the room." - Jeff Bezos, founder of Amazon. What message does your business share? How does it make them feel?
How do they feel when they see your name pop up on their screen or if they receive an email from you or your name comes up in conversation? This is essentially what a brand is, how it makes people feel. It is a fine art and the hardest work you will need to put in to create a positive brand for yourself. You essentially become an extension of your company and people will associate you with your business and vice versa. Where do you start?
I like to ask my existing clients first what their experience with my company has been and their level of satisfaction with me, my product, communication, quality, and price. I then ask the hard questions, "what should I improve on and what other products or services would you like me to offer you?".
This will probably be your best indication as to what is not working in your business and what you can improve on. It might even show you what other offerings you could add, some you might never have thought about before. I then like to conduct a survey with people that should have heard about my business but are perhaps not existing clients. I ask them if they have ever heard of my business before and if they know what I offer. If they do, then what do you think? I find out if they would ever be interested in working with me and regardless of the answer, why or why not. This is your chance to improve in a big way. Oh, and by the way, please offer them a little freebie or thank you gift for filling in the survey. Most people hate surveys unless there is something in it for them. This way, at least you will get a response.
So now you know what your customers and even strangers think of you. Now you need to create an effective marketing campaign to get your clearly defined and focused message out there. You also need to establish what you want to achieve with this message. Is it to create

a brand or a name for yourself? Is it to create more immediate sales? Is it to attract loyal clients? Make sure you know what you want your campaign to achieve and keep that end goal in mind.

Marketing, sales and branding often get lumped in the same category; however, they are so vastly different, and each has a distinctly different function. Marketing is about the company and how you want to be perceived by the customer, whereas branding is about the customer and what they think about you. Sales on the other hand are simply, bums in seats or how many tickets you have sold. If your marketing and branding are done with care and precision, then sales will happen almost automatically. Branding is the long the marathon and marketing is the sprint.

So how do you brand yourself?

First, figure out what you stand for. What is the essence of what you do? Are you here to offer a solution to the world or just in it to make money? Is your product and service good quality? Is it honest and trustworthy? What emotion does it create in your customer? Is it easily recognisable? The first thing I did when I opened 'Your Money' was having it affiliated with successful people. I launched my business and then invited celebrities to my event where I took a lot of photos of them with my brand. This is called strong brand association.

I then chose a charity I felt strongly about and supported them through hosting fundraising events and inviting my contacts to support them too. Build a good relationship with the media. Treat them with respect and invite them to these events and launches. Ask them if they perhaps need content and then supply them with a weekly or monthly article that they can use as fillers when needed.

Host free workshops to support those in need of help. Become the leader and voice on a subject related to your business.

Find groups and communities where you can provide advice and help grow your network. Enter local awards for your company. This is a great way to gain trust and recognition. Always be consistent, positive, and uplifting.

Attend important events where you know your customer and competitor will be and network like a pro.

Do a lot of kind things for people like free mentorship, products etc but do not tell people. Wait until it comes out and they all start talking about it.

It is a marathon, not a sprint, so be patient, stay humble and remember to love what you do.

It was close to the end of 'Your Money' when I realised that people were buying from me not because they thought my newspaper was the best or that I put the best events together, but because they enjoyed me as a person. I was deeply disturbed by this as I felt that people felt sorry for me and that must be why they had chosen to work with me, not because my product was great.

I felt hurt and humiliated. If only I had used that knowledge to my advantage, things would have been different but instead, I chose to rather feel sorry for myself and failed. In hindsight, it was an honour that people chose me simply because they enjoyed being around me and they enjoyed my work ethics. I was too proud to make it work for me and appreciate what was offered to me, but it was a life lesson and I try to always learn from my past mistakes and not repeat them.

It was shortly after the closure of my business that I opened that dreaded coffee shop. I was depressed as hell and made a humongous mistake.

DAY 14: RELEASE

Today is a big day.
List all the things that bother you.
Everyone that hurt you in the past, things you struggle to let go of and things you hate about yourself. List them all.
It might become emotional, which is perfectly fine, tears are the best medicine.
Once you have written them all down, find a fireproof bowl and burn the piece of paper you wrote on.
(Caution: Please be careful and use common sense so as not to become a fire hazard.)
If you have a candle and incense stick nearby, light them up and give thanks to the Universe, God, Source, yourself, whatever you believe in.
Visualise your worries, pain and anger go up in flames and feel the relief of the first step of cutting your chords with karma. It is gone, it is no longer yours. Do not take it back later. It is gone.
Wash your hands and face and feel the gratitude of the pain being washed away from you.

Add one thing you are grateful for. Close your eye and feel the joy.

Positive affirmation: "I let go of all hate and resentment. I set myself free."

CHAPTER FOURTEEN
THE HOUSE OF HORRORS -
I.E THE COFFEE SHOP

I had no newspaper.

I had small contracts here and there and far too much time on my hands. My desperate husband asked me; "What would make you happy?" and I said, "Having a coffee shop".

So, we took our savings, asked for a loan from the bank, and found a venue in a popular suburb. My idea was to have a coffee shop on the one side, a salon and beauty spa on the other, and then a play-den at the back that parents could book their children into while they enjoyed their pamper sessions. The kids had PlayStation games, puppet-shows, build-a-pizza and loads of other activities to keep them busy. We decorated the venue and then started building the pizza oven. Oh, my insanity, this Fu&*#^g pizza oven.

I had some random guy who I had found on gumtree make our furniture from scratch. I knew we had to have enough money for at least six months' rent to make sure we made it. I found companies that donated pallets to us, we just had to pick them up, so our backyard was covered with pallets. And I found some people who were looking for work to strip the pallets and sand them down. Then, the magical Dick (short for Richard) from gumtree, made benches, tables, and chairs for us. I feel sick to my stomach just thinking back to this time. It was one big blurry nightmare.

The furniture was not too bad, to be honest, the plan was rock solid, but then I had my idea to have a built-in pizza oven as I believed that would make ALLLL the difference in the world.

Our wonderful, lovely, smoky pizza oven. We spent a small fortune on cement, normal bricks, fireproof bricks, a certain type of sand, cellophane sheets, and the list went on.

While Dick was building the pizza oven, I was overseeing the guys stripping and sanding the pallets, and running to the hardware shop every five minutes because they forgot thinners, or nails, or staplers, or glue or something else. I almost went nuts!

Overnight, I had become a foreman or project manager on this construction site, and I had to watch them all the time because if I just took half a day off, nothing would have been done.

In the meantime, I was also looking for a chef and could not find one that I really wanted, so I had to just settle on one I could afford. Oh, my goodness, I almost forgot about the kitchen equipment.

I spent another small fortune on kitchen equipment, from steel tables, pots, stoves, coffee machines, crockery, and a fridge.

The fridge was so old, in the first week that I opened shop it broke and all the food inside it went off. The food constantly went off, as we barely had orders, but we still had to buy the stock just in case someone did come in. Then, on our opening night, I found heat coming from the kids play-den and upon closer inspection, I realised it was the pizza oven burning up the walls, so we had to break the entire pizza oven down.

I was broken! I kept repeating myself and changing the topic halfway through. My psychologist threatened to institutionalise me if I did not take some time off from the coffee shop. My poor husband would work half of the day at his business, and then go to the coffee shop and oversee the guys there for the rest of the day.

My beautiful friend Claire also went to run the coffee shop some evenings. Eventually, I was allowed back, and I did not want any more advice, so we ordered more bricks, sand, cement, and insulation to make an even bigger and better pizza oven.

I thought the second time round that our pizza oven would be bigger and better, and we would be able to recoup all the monies we lost as soon as we started selling these magical pizzas.

Eventually, our chef left, and our magical Dick (the Gumtree guy) became our chef. I know, it was insane.

My partner who was running the beauty salon then told me she wanted out as she was being promoted at work and did not have enough time to invest in the business any longer.

Our carpenter, pizza oven builder, chef, and manager - Dick, eventually ran away with some of our cash. It was just the craziest time we had ever been through and I went from six months' rent, down to three months' rent.

On February the third, I hosted a business networking session and called my landlord and said, "I am broke, I am out, sorry."

The poor lady was terribly upset and all I could offer her was the last months' rent after selling my equipment.
It was hell, but I felt like I escaped Alcatraz.
Shortly thereafter I started working for a beautiful organisation which I adored, but the entrepreneur in me got the better of me.

DAY 15:
PURPOSE

Today I want you to find your joy and purpose.
Think of all the things that made you happy as a child, teenager, or young adult.
You chose the life you are living, so you might need to rethink your path. Is this the way you want to continue forever?
What excites you? What makes you giddy and happy at the slightest thought?
Are you doing that? If not, why not?

I was always an incredibly happy person, but for the last six years, I was miserable. I had to dig deep and try to remember what made me happy. It was not anything big, just the simple act of feeling grateful for what I do have.
Upon waking and before I fall asleep, I give thanks for all I have.
I started my gratitude journal again. I now swear by it, it is the only thing that lifts me out of my funk.

Add one thing you are grateful for. Close your eyes and feel the joy.

Positive affirmation: "I give thanks for all I have. My supply never runs out."

CHAPTER FIFTEEN
RAISING CHILDREN

It is the greatest honour bestowed upon us. Children are like little angels. They are here to remind us of the magic and goodness in and around us.

They are little mirrors showing us who we are and what we are capable of. And of course– honesty. There are no more honest words than those spoken from a child. They do not understand deception. They love unconditionally, even if we treat them badly, they continue to love us. There is no greater sin in the world than hurting a child.

When I was younger, I used to say, "People that hurt children should be punished to death. End of story."

I explained it would be like going through a traffic light, you get flashed instantly and receive a fine. Similarly, when you hurt a child, you get flashed instantly and struck dead. No court case, no lawyers or judges, just instant death. I have mellowed a ton since my outspoken youth days. I did warn you, I am not always the nicest person on earth, but I do believe the world would be a much better place to be in if those that hurt the innocent

- children, animals, and the weak - were dealt with more severely. But I must admit, it is hard to raise children.

During the first two years of James' life, Paul and I barely slept a wink. We were like walking zombies. I do not know or understand how we raised a little boy, with both of us starting our businesses at the same time and being newly together, and still here to tell the story. It was d-i-f-f-i-c-u-l-t! James was an especially difficult boy to raise until his sister arrived. He was a colic baby and would cry throughout the night.

He was incredibly strong-willed, and it was hard not to give in. We were the only ones in our group of friends who had a child, so we just had to wing it. We did not know anything about raising a child. All we knew was – we needed to make sure he was safe – check, we needed to make sure he was eating – check and we needed to make sure he received lots of love – check. The rest we made up as we went along.

We were told that James needed more discipline and that he was going to be a maniac killer one day. He was wild. He cracked my nose when he was two years old while we were play fighting, and he kicked me in the face so hard that my nose cracked.

There was not a toy that was not broken, even our pot plants outside were not safe. At one point we were concerned as to whether we should get help or what we should be doing differently, but Paul was adamant that James was fine. He said the boy was simply strong-willed and that he would grow out of it.

He did not want to temper the boy's fiery nature as although James is very strong-willed, he is also kind and caring and has a soft heart, so we let him run wild for a bit.

My beautiful dad and Paul would often debate the topic of nature versus nurture. Paul believes in nature and my dad and I believe in nurture. Paul would say that James is the kind and strong-willed boy that he is because that is the way he was born. My dad and I would say that he is kind and strong-willed due to the way we brought him up. The jury is still out, and I think you can all agree that this is a hot and interesting topic around the fire.

Now that I am older, I understand that James was just acting out as he had no routine and structure in his life. Paul and I were poor for the first two years of being together which coincides with James's life. We moved to seven different houses during that time. I remember my cousin telling his sister at our fifth housewarming party that he was not going to come anymore as he cannot keep tabs on where we are and when we will be moving again.

It was nuts, but we made it. Our secret, I think, was that we kept being playful. We did not take life too seriously and had fun just being together, appreciating what we did have – each other. What I learned is that all a child really needs is love and protection and routine.

They want your time, not gifts. In hindsight, I also realised that we did not feed our boy well enough. He would have sweets almost every day, drink flavoured juice and sleep whenever it suited us.

I just changed these two things with Bella (my daughters) routine and saw a major difference in her behaviour.

Sugar and artificial flavourings cause hyperactivity and can cause or worsen behavioural problems such as ADHD. You will hear your grandparents often say, that they never experienced these modern illnesses or behavioural problems that we experience today.

It is largely because they ate better. They did not eat processed food or have artificial sweeteners and flavourings. They slept when it was dark and woke up when it was light.

These two things are so crucial for their development and we were bad parents because we lacked the education and experience needed to raise a healthy, happy child.

On this topic, I genuinely believe we have an ability to heal our bodies and rid it of dis-ease. I recently became a qualified NADA Acupuncture Practitioner. It is the placement of 5 needles in each ear (Sympathetic – strong relaxant effect on organs, Shen Men – alleviates anxiety and nervous system, Kidney – Influence mental state and relieves fear also increase your willpower, Liver – Resolves anger and aggression and lastly the Lungs – aiding respiration and protecting the body from disease, detoxification and release sadness and control.) It was designed to treat addicts and Post Traumatic Stress Disorders (PTSD). It even helps cancer patients, insomniacs, migraine sufferers, ADHD, hormonal imbalances, endometriosis, diabetes, and depression, and the list just goes and on and on. It is the best treatment I have ever had in my life by the way.

It changed my behaviour and addictive personality. I still give myself a treatment once a week and my darling husband, who grins and bears it with me.

All these artificial food and flavours, and even negative emotions cause poisons in our bodies. Dis – ease is just that. Your body is not at ease with the poisons in it and so it causes disease and illness.

According to research done on the link between cancer and emotional trauma, they discovered that most of their patients harboured similar emotional triggers according to where the cancer was.

For instance, cancers found in the bones: would be lack of self-worth, brain: stubbornness, breast tissue (duct): separation conflict, cervix: frustration, lungs: fear of dying and melanoma: feeling dirty.

High levels of sugar content perhaps caused by depleted adrenaline can cause normal cells to become cancerous.

Therefore, it is important to detox your body of the poisons we knowingly or unwittingly induce. Another great natural remedy is to have a spoonful of Bicarbonate of Soda (dissolved in a little water) once a day.

It helps to neutralise sugars and alkaline your body.

Do yourself a favour and find a local NADA Detox Practitioner close by and get a few treatments. You could start with once a week, or if your condition is more serious, have two treatments a week for at least three months. The results are astounding, but you must stick to the treatments.

I digress – again, apologies. This monkey-mind of mine runs at the speed of light in all different directions – all the time!

After years of trial and error – we eventually near-perfected the art of parenting. (Well, we like to think we did. We are waiting with bated breath when they become teenagers). We have become strict parents; we do not tolerate disrespect or bad manners.

We have a basic routine we live by, and we strongly believe that every member of the household should be allowed to have his own opinion and must be heard. We believe in fairness and trust and we shower each other with kindness, love, and support.

We do not use negative words to define a person, for instance, when the children are naughty, we say, "what you did was naughty", not "You are a very naughty child".

We explain to them why we are punishing them, and sometimes take away a toy or the television for a while. We do not a always have enough money to buy the things that the children want, but we never say, "We don't have money", or "Money doesn't grow on trees" (which creates a scarcity mindset).

We would rather say something like, "Great, now we know what you want, we will put it on the wish list and let you know as soon as it is time to achieve it". Or we will give them a list of chores to do and after that period has passed, they can have their item of choice. We are firm believers that abundance is everywhere and that you can have anything you want, just make sure you truly do want it – then release.

I sometimes fear sending my children into the world.

The youth of today have become self-entitled and think that the world owes them everything. The fact is the world does not owe us anything. If you want something, then go out there and get it.

We are meant to create our realities, not to wait until life dishes out what you lazily thought of. We are meant to be purposeful creators of our worlds, to be the light. We are so precious and unbelievably beautiful; we just need to allow ourselves to shine!

I have noticed with increasing dismay how readily we give in to the demands of our children.

We look away when we see their disrespectful behaviour. Perhaps out of fear that they will not love us if we reprimand them. But what we forget is that our children are not our friends, they are our children, and we are their parents.

We are meant to guide them and raise them to be superior beings, to be better than we are, to give them the self-confidence to go out there and explore the world, not bully their way into it or cower behind our skirts. It is our responsibility to raise good, healthy, kind, and loving children that respect themselves and others.

It is our responsibility to teach them the difference between right and wrong and allow them to be self-reliant and possess the ingrained principles of being a decent human being.
Like my dad always says, "There is no such thing as a naughty child, only a naughty parent".
It is never too late to take back our power; step up the parenting game and be just that – a parent.
It is up to us to make and create a good and happy life for them and our family.

On this note, I want to give a special mention to all the single parents out there. You amaze me. I honestly can not imagine doing this entire parenting thing on my own. How do you do it?
You work all day and probably weekends too, as your pay goes to feeding your family. You spend every waking minute caring for your children, preparing the food, creating a safe environment for them, giving them love and attention, and being the disciplinarian, the teacher, the mother, the father, the friend, the everything.
I get tired just thinking about it. But you do it, every single day, without a break, without a complaint, without help.
I was about to proclaim an international Single Parent Day and then I saw, Ronald Reagan already jumped the gun – in 1984.
In America, you celebrate these superhuman heroes on 21 March - nice.
In South Africa, we celebrate Human Rights Day on this day. But I am sure we can squeeze in another celebration for these unsung heroes or better yet, for an hour each day, we celebrate you. I do not know about other countries, but in South Africa, single-parent households (normally single mothers) are prevalent.
And the thing that fills me with such fury, is the lack of support for them, and even the accusing glances and whispers behind the married couples' hands.
I am not going to make a generalisation here and say all single women are left by lying sacks of useless shits, but if the shoe fits, then please be my guest and put it on. Every situation is different, but I can not understand how we can live in a modern society where we still frown upon a single mother raising her child – instead of treating her like royalty and showering her with admiration and gifts.
No, instead we become bias and accuse her of being a harlot, she must have brought it upon herself, she wanted to do the deed, so she must live with the consequences.
Excuse me for a second, but did immaculate conception just take place? Was she filled with the spirit of God and able to produce a child on her own? No.

On the other side of the bed, there was a man who longed for the warmth and comfort that a woman provides.

Perhaps sweet nothings and empty promises were whispered in her ears – and then nine months later, conveniently forgotten.

Ladies, if the father of your child is not in your life during your pregnancy, chances are highly unlikely that he will be there for you after birth. You need to think hard about your life ahead.

Do you include him on the birth certificate, do you give the child his surname, are you going to push for maintenance?

Remember, if he is on the birth certificate, you will never be able to travel or move abroad or make important decisions without his signed approval. It is a decision only you can make, but make sure you make an informed one, based on expert guidance and trust your gut, you are never wrong and know exactly what to do. I salute you!

When Bella was born, James became a meek, little puppy.

He instantly calmed down and became a very attentive brother who adored his sister. They are still the best of friends and enjoy spending time together. Bella was the easiest baby ever.

I would feed her, and she would fall asleep instantly, only waking up six hours later. She was a dream. No crying at night, no niggles, simply perfect, but God, was I depressed.

I wished someone had warned us how different life would be once we became four instead of three. The dynamics of the relationship between all parties changed and I for one had the baby blues.

I eventually reached a floor level low and was experiencing depression for the first time in my life. My hormones were all over the place. My pretty curly, copper hair turned nearly black with strings of grey in between. It was thick and hard, and my feet grew a size bigger.

It could also be that for once, I was taking life a little slower than the usual eighteen-hour workdays I was used to.

Two months after I gave birth to my girl, I broke my leg in three places – it was horrendously painful.

Another hard lesson I learned here. If you get a nudge to change or move something, do it, do not delay, as it is your inner guidance trying to protect you.

We bought our property two months before I gave birth to Bella and we had lots to do to make it liveable. We repainted the entire place, fixed the floorboards, re-did the garden, prepared for the baby, worked on our businesses and looked after our boy.

In our garden, we removed the pavers and only paved one-third of it but the section right under the patio did not fit together properly. The week before my fall, I stepped into a tiny hole between the two pavers and sprained my ankle. I told my husband we needed to fix that, but alas - we did not.

The following Sunday, my husband had to go to his workshop to finish an urgent order and left his keys at home. When he returned by lunchtime, he buzzed the gate for me to let him in.

I walked outside as the inside buzzer was not working; with Bella on my hip, and I stepped down.

With the added weight I was holding and most of the nutrients in my body being used to feed my baby, I stepped in that same hole from the week prior, twisted my ankle and fell on my leg, breaking it in three different places.

To top it all off, I dropped my poor baby and she was screaming her little lungs out and I nearly passed out from the pain - with my husband staring at us in desperation as he was locked outside the gate.

Luckily one of our neighbours in our complex was home and came to our aid; let Paul in and called the ambulance. So next time that little voice tells you to do something – just do it.

I love being a mother, I honestly do, I love nothing more than spending all my free time with my children, but I also love the hustle of work. I was so excited that I could get back to work after giving birth, but then I broke my leg. I could not move for two months and by then it was nearly the end of the year and no one wanted to see me, so I could only return to work nearly a year after giving birth. I was miserable and deeply depressed, even manic come to think of it. There was no talk about this during my baby's check-ups, there were no discussions about what to do if you feel like that. If this sounds familiar to you, please seek help as it is completely natural. Your hormones are just out of whack and you are trying to cope with a new baby.

I even felt disconnected from her, like she was not real to me.

Belinda suggested I take Espiride just to take the edge off and it worked. I do not know how I would have coped without those little anti-depressants. I wished there were more articles and warnings about having your second baby. Everything changes.

Your home dynamics, your relationship with your husband, your firstborn, yourself - everything. It was difficult.

Drinking did not help and neither did the fact that I had just used all our life savings and made more debt opening a coffee shop - which I had to close with R400 000 worth of debt.

My husband was frantic and did not know what to do with me anymore. I was irrational. I was seeing a psychologist who kept saying I needed to slow down and meditate, take time out for myself. I thought he was an idiot; how could he tell me to slow down when I had so much to do. I did not dare sit down, because then the carefully crafted life I had created in my mind would come tumbling down and I did not want that.

I had already felt the pinch from sitting around doing nothing when my leg was broken, I was not going to go down that road again.

The thing about depression is that no-one can lift you out of it.

It must come from you. You have to be the one to decide to say, "I do not want this life anymore. I want things to change", and then be willing to put in the work to change your life. Choose to make the change or accept the life you have.

But before all of this, you might need help. Sometimes depression stems from a chemical imbalance in your body, and that can easily be rectified if you get support. I now know I could have healed myself, but at the time, I did not know the power I have and needed the chemicals to help me deal with life.

DAY 16:
SPOIL YOURSELF

Today, go out and do something special just for yourself.

Whether it is an hour-long bubble bath with a glass of wine and music, buying yourself that cute pair of shoes or simply taking that nap.
Learn to treat yourself, putting you first.
If you struggle with this, imagine you are planning a very special treat for your best friend or child, then plan it and go and enjoy your treats.

Write down what you are going to do or have done for yourself today.

Add one thing you are grateful for. Close your eyes and feel the joy.

Positive affirmation: "I deserve abundance and joy. I am worthy of receiving."

CHAPTER SIXTEEN
MARRIAGE

Marriage is sacred. What few of us remember is that we swear in front of God that we will treasure this person and love them and care for them till the end of days.

Yes, I get it, we meet our loves, fall head over heels, and decide that we want to be with that person forever or our hearts will simply break into millions of pieces.

But then the honeymoon period fades, and we see each other for what we are, warts and all, and it is not a pretty sight.

The things we loved about them, their little quirks, become our biggest irritation so we get it in our minds that we want to change them to suit our needs.

Can you remember when last you tried to change yourself?

It is almost impossible, but you still want to go and change someone else. Well, let me let you in on a little secret. You are not going to change that person. What you see in front of you is what you are going to get for life. They might change little ways, small habits, but what you see is what you get.

My aunt used to say marriage was hard work. You needed to see it like any other one of your work obligations. What you put in; you will get out. For a long time, my husband and I placed each other on a pedestal and refused to see each other's flaws. And then, once the honeymoon period ended, all those cute little things we used to love about each other became intolerable and annoying. I do not think either of us realised that we idealised each other to death. It was unrealistic and we had built such high expectations of each other that it became impossible to live up to.

I used to look at Paul secretly and wonder, "When is he going to wake up and realise how amazing he is and what a shitty person I am?".

I simply loved the way he loved me.

I felt like a goddess, he made me feel invincible and untouchable, like I could do and have anything. He loved me so hard that the ice around my heart started to melt and I felt free to love him in return, and even to start loving myself again. I needed it. I needed to feel loved and worthy and fabulous. Everyone deserves a love like this. In return, I loved and adored him just as hard and expected so much from him.

I literally would not have been surprised if he told me one day that he was a semi-god. He was God's gift to me, until one day, he did a very ordinary thing. For other people, it would be normal, but for me it was devastating. My beautiful prince came tumbling down from the throne I had placed him on, and the thin veil of glass broke and shattered into millions of pieces.

The glass was my impossible perception of him. No one is perfect, it is why we are called human – we are fallible, we fall, we break, we make mistakes and so we learn. I did not get it.

Not only did he fall off the pedestal I had put him on, but how I saw myself through his eyes changed, and God was she ugly.

I could not stand to look at myself, and I blamed him.

It was his fault for getting off his pedestal and it was also his fault that I had to see myself for who I truly was.

I felt like an ugly green monster and I became this creation in my mind. This was also during my baby blues, so I was already depressed from hormone imbalances, with a broken leg, which made me feel even more vulnerable and dependant on him.

I do not know if all women are like me, but I enjoyed being perceived as superwoman. I would get up early, prepare the kids lunches, get their porridge ready, wake them up, get them ready for school, get myself ready, take them to school, go to work, pick them up from school, make the dinner, clean the house and then I maybe had 30 minutes left for my husband, but none for me, that was unheard of. I did not understand the concept of taking time for myself. I had to stay so damn busy for me not to think.

It was part of my turning point though and it had to happen.

I had to learn to trust Paul with household chores. I hated the way he cleaned the house and made the food and packed the lunches, but I had to learn to just shut up and smile and thank him for trying.

So, my perfect little world crumbled into pieces, but in return, I learned to let go and trust my husband to do things for me.

I am a carer and I always want to care for others, but it is so hard for me to accept help from others. This taught me to also allow Paul to care for me. I did not know how much concealed resentment I had for him, as I would constantly think of how much I did in the house and how little he did.

When this came out, he was surprised as he thought he was doing enough. This perfect little bubble we created for each other, popped, and, in its place, we grew closer and into having a more stable and mature relationship. One where we had an equal partnership and responsibility to work on our relationship and family.

We saw each other as equals, but it did not happen overnight.

At first, we insisted that the one partner needed to make the other partner happy, "You don't make me happy anymore" or, "What do you do to make me happy?" or, "You have changed so much, I don't know you anymore".

There were too many of those instances to count.

We would take a few weeks holiday away from each other, just to learn to breathe by ourselves again.

When you live with each other, you tend to almost become one other. You live on top of each other and barely have space and time to be by yourself. And just for the record, no one is supposed to make you happy. It is not your husband or wife's responsibility, only you can make yourself happy. You can try to make each other's lives easier, more bearable, pleasant, and fun, but you cannot make someone happy. Happiness comes from within.

If you are an unhappy person, then it does not matter if you marry the most perfect, handsome, prettiest, or richest person, you will still be unhappy, and only you can change that.

It is not fair to demand happiness from your partner; it just adds additional and unnecessary stress on the relationship. We are so vastly different from one another.

One day in a heated argument, Paul said, "You stand at the edge of a cliff looking down and you think, lets jump, but you don't have a parachute or anything prepared, you just think you have a good idea and everything will just appear like magic. You don't think about how you are going to do it; or what the consequences will be, you just think I want it and I want it now." So I screamed back at him, "Yes, and you just stand there making calculations of how far down the jump will be, then you go back to the house and make plans of how you are going to do it, and then one month later, you might go out and buy the equipment, but by that time, I already jumped and am back at home".

Then he said, "Yes with broken limbs" and I said, "Well at least I did it!". And this summed up our relationship.

Paul is the shyest person you will ever meet and has low energy. He is cautious and likes to do things in his own time. I, on the other hand, am impulsive and outgoing. I enjoy mingling with loads of people and if I have an inspired idea, I want to implement it immediately. I am impatient and want to do a lot of different things at once. I have high energy, so we were often at war, normally the silent kind, where we ignored each other for days on end and then he would get fed up and want to talk and I would rather just shout.

I still have not learned how to argue with him. I am shit at it.

But we managed to get through it. When I had my breakdown, I was impossible to handle, and would not stop drinking.

We went to so many counsellors and nothing helped because I was not ready to be helped. In a relationship, you need to set boundaries as to what is acceptable and what is not and if those lines are crossed, you need to decide if it is what you signed up for, or if you are worth more. My husband knew the kids and he deserved more and said to me, "Get help or ship out".

I am all for fighting for your relationship and I truly do believe that 90% of relationships are worth saving, but you should never become a broken version of yourself to save your relationship.

I believe the reason Paul and I are still together is his persistence to communicate with me. I still struggle to this day to openly share my feelings with him as I am either scared that I will hurt his feelings, or I am just hurt and not ready to speak about it.

Another thing we have never let go of is our respect for each other. Even in our most heated arguments, will we not say ugly things about each other's body or character. We fight about how we make each other feel and what we did that upset the other, but we do not go into each other's character. Those words will stay with you forever so rather do not do that

– ever!

DAY 17:
CHARITY

Do something nice for someone without telling anyone.

It can be anything you can think of.
Just go out there and do something nice for someone, without expecting anything in return or even better, without them knowing it was you.
It can be buying groceries for a family you know are struggling and just leaving it on their porch or donating money to a stray dog, whatever it is, just do something selfless today.
There are two things I want you to learn or realise here. The first one is that other You can write it down in your diary.
Add one thing you are grateful for. Close your eyes and feel the joy.

Positive affirmation: "I am love divine. I share my many blessings with love."

CHAPTER SEVENTEEN
SOBER UP - IT IS GOING TO
BE A BUMPY RIDE (2017)

It will be three years in September 2020 since I had my last drink and smoke. I am still so proud of this.

I am deeply grateful that I do not have cravings for alcohol.

This was one of my gravest fears when I first stopped. I was concerned that the cravings would overpower me, but so far, I have only had one moment when I so desperately wanted to cave in.

This was before we moved to Scotland.

My husband just held me that night as I cried and shouted and bemoaned my life. The next morning, everything was back to normal. The same however cannot be said about smoking. I miss those little devils like I miss a day on the beach. I can still taste it; smell it and remember the elation when I inhaled and exhaled each puff.

It was like my whole world would stand still for a second and it was just me and the universe.

The relief and pleasure were like nothing I have ever experienced before. I was a bit of a chain-smoker and would smoke between twenty and forty cigarettes a day. It is no wonder I still forget to breathe sometimes. I often find myself gasping for air and then feel such relief when I get a deep, full breath of air in my lungs and the almost painful exhale. Yeah, I think my lungs are still in recovery after the years of abuse. According to statistics, my risk for coronary heart disease decreases by half after one year and after five years without smoking, the body has healed itself enough for the arteries and blood vessels to begin to widen again. I guess I still have a long road ahead of me.

My self-indulgent 'treat' is now a little getaway with my family. It costs less than it would have cost us for a month of drinking and smoking plus the aftereffects of a hangover aka junk food! Since then, every time I felt like a cigarette, we packed up the car and went away for the weekend.

Except when Covid-19 arrived in full force and banned us from going anywhere, but that is for another chapter all on its own.

We did manage to go to Brussels and Waterloo in Belgium while we lived in the Netherlands.

It was such an exhilarating experience. You simply pack the car and three hours later you ended up in another country, and a beautiful country to boot.

Back to the booze.

My relationship with alcohol started when I was ten years old.

It was at my sisters sixteenth birthday celebration when I could have a glass of champagne. I liked it so much, I even had my other sister's glass and perhaps even more, who knows. All I remember was how beautiful everything looked. I remember the buzz, the giggles, the light-headedness and the courage and confidence I had.

Everything looked, smelled, and tasted better. I felt alive. So alive!

Scientists say that alcohol abuse is hereditary but agree that it mostly stems from experiencing a traumatic childhood.

Another interesting study was on a region in the brain called the Lateral Habenula, associated with making decisions and learning about punishments. If this part of the brain is not active, then decision-making skills and fear of punishment is not too strong.

The study found that this part of the brain is not active in most addicts, but they have not assessed yet if it is something you are born with or if trauma can inhibit the use of this region.

That first buzz got me hooked on cigarettes too. I would steal my stepmother's cigarettes whenever I had the chance and indulge in the 'treat' until I had the opportunity to get my hands on some alcohol without any adults noticing. The secret was in making myself useful to them by pouring their drinks and serving snacks. Then once they were on their way it was as easy as baking pie to steal their alcohol.

The rush, oh my heavens, it was the rush I was after.

The feeling of butterflies in my stomach when I knew I was going to have a party later that day or when I woke up just knowing it was going to be a great day because it was Friday, and I would be going out for a few beers and maybe some wine by lunchtime.

Everything I ever did I planned around my drinking habit.

I would make sure that I had extra bottles of wine if I knew a friend was coming over. I would schedule late meetings for the following day if I knew I was going to have more than my fair share of alcohol that evening. I would make sure that I did not see important clients on the days I knew I would have a hangover, those would be my admin days, and I had lots of them. I was however mostly happy.

I was carefree, I loved life, I was exuberant and joyful, and had a lust for life. The world was my oyster... for as long as I had booze in my cupboard.

I later discovered that alcohol can be detected in your hair for up to ninety days after your last drink. This was normally the longest I could make it without alcohol or a cigarette.

My cravings would normally become severe after two days of not drinking. I hated feeling normal, so I would find an excuse to have a drink again before the demon came out to play.

This darkness inside of me would always come out by the 4th or 5th glass, which occurred most nights. I would pick a fight with anyone close to me, usually my husband. I would then feel so incredibly sad, angry, and hurt; I would just cry and cry until I fell asleep.

This monster inside of me always had to be fed, but not too much, I just could not figure out the balance.

I have always been amazed at how people can just have one or two drinks at a party and then have a glass of coke. In my mind, it was a superhuman strength that they possessed. It was never enough for me. Even if I had too much wine the night before, I would be ready for the next session the following evening, and it would never be two glasses followed by coke either.

I was thirty-six years old when I lost my business, I almost lost my husband and most importantly, I lost my self-respect.

I hated who I had become when the booze demon had its fill.

I tried to stop drinking so many times, it became an annual thing, where I would stop for a week or two, and sometimes make it to three months, but then the demon would be crawling up my neck and insist that it was my friend. I fought it so many times, I would have plea-bargained with it, begging it to allow me to only drink on weekends. Or, if I had to, only have two glasses a night.

But I was a proper addict, and I did not know how to stop.

The turning point came after I lost the coffee shop. I was a little psychotic and my thoughts became suicidal.

I remember driving home one night with the family in the car.

It was unusual for me to drink and drive as I would always get 'Home James' or an 'Uber', but this night I decided to drive myself. I was driving down the highway and it was about 10 meters before I had to turn left.

I did not break and just kept driving, thinking it was best to end it all. I thought perhaps it was better if they all died with me.

It was so dark inside of me, my mind was scrambled, and my heart was loaded.

I have been thinking a lot about my mother's suicide and my childhood.

I felt sorry for myself and my husband had his hands full trying to keep our family together.

I felt alone and misunderstood, I was in severe pain and I genuinely believed that alcohol would help me cope with all these emotions. Of course, it did not, it never does, it always makes it worse.

As the seconds ticked past, a force bigger than me overpowered me and I turned left, avoiding going over the highway and nose-diving into the ocean.

My heart was thumping like a jackhammer in my chest, my ears were ringing, and I struggled to keep the steering wheel straight on the road. My whole body was shaking like a leaf.

Our home was close by and I parked to get my family out.

I cannot begin to tell you how deeply ashamed I felt that very minute. The self-loathing and utter disgust I had for myself made me physically nauseous that night.

I knew within every corner and fibre of my body that I had to stop or my family or I would die.

For the first time, I became aware of how selfish I had been towards myself and my family and how I was self-sabotaging.

I phoned the suicide helpline the next day and they tried to talk sense into me and told me that I needed help.

I went to see a psychologist and explained how drinking a few glasses helped me cope with life.

I did not tell her the whole story and she said it was fine, and that I could have a few glasses with no harm.

You see, when you are not drinking you do and say anything to get permission and access to your next kick.

You lie and steal and hurt anyone that stands in your way.

What became evident was the way I had learned to lie to myself to try and hide the truth from myself. I knew deep down inside that I was addicted and needed help, I was just feeding myself little lies to drag it out for as long as I could.

It took a further two months and numerous threats from my husband that he would leave me if I did not stop drinking.

I considered going to AA, but no one really knew that I was an alcoholic.

I felt I knew too many people in my city, and I was far too proud to ask for help, it would be shameful for me and my family. What would people think of me?

So, I found my own way out. I had been wanting to stop smoking for years too and it seemed more socially acceptable to admit that you are addicted to smoking. Wanting to stop smoking is seen as a huge achievement and everyone cheers you on.

"Yeah, you can do it! Well done for stopping! It is the best thing you can ever do for yourself".

"Hi guys, I am on day five and I feel great, taking it day by day".

All these words of encouragement you see on your social media pages with happy smiley faces but mention the alcohol and the feedback disappears.

I do not know if it is because of guilt that most people fear they may have an alcohol problem too, but alcoholics and drug addicts are always perceived in a dirtier way.

Like, "Ooh so and so is an alcoholic. She brought it upon herself, she should just not drink so much" or "He is a coke addict, he is so stupid. He cannot even afford food, but he wants to buy coke. I don't understand why he doesn't just stop." Like we choose to be addicts and ruin our lives!?

There is no, "You go girl, you can do it, well done, this is the best thing you can do for yourself". Nope.

There is just silence and judgment.

People treat you differently if they know you were an addict, like you are broken and fragile.

They mostly just avoid you and the topic. I find it very condescending, but I guess I was the same when I was drinking if a friend of mine stopped. I would avoid them as I felt guilty for wanting alcohol myself. It made me feel weak and a lessor person for drinking in their presence.

So, I found a way out of my dilemma by concocting my plan where I could stop both and just blame it on the cigarettes. That way I could also get the comments, "You go girl, you can do it, it's the best thing you can do for yourself" etc.

I found Alan Carr's 'Stop Smoking' ad online and decided to buy it. It was Sunday the 2nd of September 2017 when I had my last farewell party with alcohol and cigarettes. I drank until my stomach could take no more and my lungs were struggling to have another smoke, but I forced myself. I knew this was my last "hoorah" and then I just cried and shouted till I had nothing left inside of me.

I feared the unknown.

I have never known a life without booze, and I was scared I would become dull and boring with nothing to look forward to in life.

I was petrified that I would simply stop existing, I did not know what to expect and I was incredibly scared of what sober life would do to me. At one point I thought it would be easier to just die than live a sober life. My husband stood by me that night and just kept consoling me, telling me how nice it was going to be, what fun things we would do, and on we went until I passed out.

I want to compare the process I went through to dealing with grief. At first, I was in denial of the magnitude of what I was going through. For years I was in denial of the severity of my addiction. Then came the searing anger, with myself, the world and everyone around me. Oh, and then the bargaining started. Boy, did I bargain with this demon inside of me. Only a few drinks on the weekend I promise, or just two glasses of wine a night. Then the deep depression sinks in when you realise that nothing is working. The feeling of being trapped and being worthless. The despair and self-hate are shattering. Then slowly but surely you come to accept your situation for what it is. The blame becomes less, and you start preparing yourself for what is to come i.e. living without alcohol. It looks dark and scary; life seems pointless and not worth living. But you know you must do it, or you will lose it all. So, the morning of the third broke upon us. I phoned in sick from my new job and my husband took off from his business. We took the kids to school, made ourselves coffee and breakfast, and started watching the Alan Carr movie. It was six hours of intense viewing. Boy was I angry. I felt so stupid. I felt betrayed. My best friends, 'cigarettes', were not my friends at all, they did not give me what I was seeking, and my party friend, 'booze' was also not quite what I made him out to be most of my life.

I felt a deep betrayal and bitter anger boiling inside of me.

DAY 18:
CHALLENGE YOURSELF

Today I want you to do something that scares you.
(But please do not put yourself in physical harm.)

I am speaking of phoning or texting the person that harmed you and telling them that what they did to you is not ok, but you have forgiven them and wish them well.
Or it could be speaking to the cute guy you work with or even just telling your children they cannot have a sweet today.
It starts small. You don't have start big until you have built up your confidence, but at least try to push your boundaries today.
List what you have done and then perhaps what you still would like to do - like a bucket list of sorts.

Add one thing you are grateful for. Close your eyes and feel the joy.

Positive affirmation: "I let go of past hurt, it no longer has control over me."

CHAPTER EIGHTEEN
THE AWAKENING

But then, the healing process started.
I was a mess. My dreams would haunt me. The shame I felt from
flashbacks of the things I had done and said was crushing. The best way
to describe it is feeling like my skin was being peeled off my body and I
was naked for everyone to see.
My childhood pain and sadness came to haunt me.
For once in my life, I had to face all my demons head-on and sober. No
more drinking to numb the pain, no more hiding from the causes. It
was judgment day, and I was found wanting.
I am not going to lie; it was the toughest thing I have ever had to do in
my entire life. But so worth it!

A month after I stopped drinking and smoking, I saw a friend offering
online guided meditation classes for twenty-one days.
We had to get up at 4 am every morning, do gentle breathing exercises,
and then she would do the most beautiful, guided meditation for
fifteen minutes, followed by a ten-minute journaling and dreaming
opportunity. I cannot describe it any better than to say I found my
bliss, pure untainted love, and peace.
It was so beautiful it made me want to cry with gratitude.
My heart was filled with this gentle, flowing grace surrounding and
carrying me. I found God / Source and my beautiful angels, and
I started to love myself again, broken and scarred, and together
we healed me.
Today, I can share my story without wanting to collapse in pain or hide
in shame. I realised how incredibly lucky and blessed I am to have
found this new path and I can say with all honesty that being sober is
the best damn gift I could ever have given myself.
I thank my sweet Creator every day for the new life I have and for
putting me back together again. I now know how beautiful and special

I am, and I hold intense gratitude for living this precious gift called life with clarity of thought.

But most of all, I am forever grateful that I still have the love and respect of my wonderful husband and that my children never have to be surrounded by that darkness ever again.

I have cut the chords with Karma and paid my debts. I am still on the road to recovery and healing.

Different issues and parts of my personality still pop up that I have not noticed before, but I have become a new person. The old Lynn died on the floor that night and a new one was reborn.

It was like learning to walk, talk, eat, and breathe again.

Right now, I am like a toddler and I am moving at a great speed.

Since I stopped drinking, I have changed my hair, my clothes, my make- up, the way I speak, my friends, and even my beliefs. I have de-aged by about ten years. My skin is brighter, my hair is shinier, my teeth are whiter, and best of all I have so much more time available to do self- improving activities and spend quality time with my family. I started making hand-stitched clothing, home-made beauty products, baking, going for long walks in nature, and of course – writing this book.

My income increased three times and my aspirations are now so big I tremble at the thought of them. I am confident in who I am.

For the first time, I know my worth and I genuinely love and respect myself. This is not something I could have said a few years ago. I loathed myself, I was deeply ashamed of how weak I was.

Today, I am strong, and I am present every day, living in the moment and appreciating life for what it is – a gift!

I found this article I wrote six months into being sober.

Shame

Such a powerful emotion and very easily enforced upon another person or yourself. Shame is what bullies and abusers use to manipulate you into doing what they want you to do against your will.

Shame is what businesses and bad managers use to get you to buy into them. So how does it work?

They use your kindness, personality, love, or desire and turn it into something ugly. You might know it is not ugly, but perhaps you are not confident enough when they attack you, so you give in and believe that what they are saying is true, and before you know it, you are overcome by shame.

Shame is then followed by remorse and when one feels remorseful, you tend to want to repent and atone for your perceived sins – and that is when they get you. The bullies/abusers succeed in making you feel remorseful and then proceed to tell you what you can do to repent – by doing what they want you to do.

For some reason, society teaches us to feel shameful for wanting money and nice things or to be pretty and popular.

Instead, we should simply be thankful for what we have and leave it at that. Well, I call bull on it.

Life is supposed to be beautiful, filled with magic and opportunities; for you to have the freedom to explore what you want in life and to go for it. If what you want is for the greater good and does not harm you or others, then what is ugly or shameful about that?

Remember there is a difference between being greedy and desiring a better life for yourself and those around you.

Learn to detect the bullies who just want to manipulate you into doing things you do not want to do for their gain.

Most bullies have experienced extreme pain and sadness in their lives and do not know how to deal with their pain.

They only know pain and shame and thus inflict it upon those around them. It is not your responsibility to accept it though, be strong, know that you are special and wonderful. You are worth it!

Being Gentle

(I wrote this nine months after I stopped drinking.)

I feel a lot, too much, and most times I do not know when it is going to happen until the tears start peeking out of the corners of my eyes.

Like an unwanted guest, they keep coming, even when I dry them angrily with my sleeves.

At first, I was ashamed of my heightened emotions and inability to speak from the heart without crying. I could not do wedding speeches, talk about my own life or those who touched my life, without a fountain of tears coming along.

I thought I was too soft and tried everything in my power to switch the floodgate of emotions off.

I drowned it in alcohol and turned it into anger as I believed that anger was better than feeling any pain and hurt. I became an angry drunk.

My husband and I decided to stop drinking nine months ago.

I packed up the cigarettes, which was the main motivator to stop both vices and we have been a perfect example of clean living since.

Well, except for the chocolates and occasional pizza and swearing...

But hey, something has got to give. I was terribly angry at myself for the first few months of clean living. I saw my wasted life for what it was – an abuse of the most beautiful God-given gift ever.

I felt ashamed of myself for being stupid enough not to notice what a slave I had been. A slave to society, to things, instant gratification, and most of all a slave to a dull mind. Since then I have become awakened. I am even more aware of things, people, and emotions than I have ever felt before. My energy field has become extremely sensitive too, I pick up on everyone's emotions and feelings around me and it affects me deeply. So deeply that I have started withdrawing from social gatherings and cancelled interactive activities with my friends and family. Well except those where if I am not present, they will disown me completely. I am like a hare that comes out of her hole occasionally to eat and say hi, then crawls back inside her warm and cosy home. My home has become my sanctuary, my husband and kids are my only source of socialising and I am so happy with this arrangement.

I joined online meditation groups and have learned how to ground my emotions and how to connect with my inner guide.

It is all too beautiful and pure, and it feels kind of scary to talk about, but I experienced bliss. That deep, warm fuzzy feeling like you are basking in adoration, love, and blessings, and feeling so incredibly happy and grateful. And, I have not even started to explain this word to you. I am now coping with external influences, outside negative energies, and an overflow of useless information.

Perhaps not what you wanted to hear, but I am not thriving in the outside world yet. However, I am coping.

I have learnt several lessons that I would like to share with you. Just remember that we are all unique and we have our own coping mechanisms.

Be gentle:

Treat yourself like you would your best friend or most loved child. You are so incredibly special and unique, do not compare yourself with other people.

Their success, stories, and life paths are so different from yours. Focus on your own beautiful life, gifts, and blessings.

Find yourself a new hobby:

I picked up needlework and baking. I always loved beautiful materials, but never knew what I wanted to do with this enjoyment. So, I bought myself some of my favourite fabric and an extremely easy pattern and I now make cute, handstitched skirts for myself and my girl every month. I bake a cake with the kids every weekend too and these are now my little pleasures.

Read up on things that excite or interest you:

I am a bit obsessive, but I have accepted it. Instead of once or twice, I do some things all the time. I start my morning with meditation and an angel reading, then I listen to motivational YouTube clips while driving to work and on my way back home. While cooking a big dinner for the next two nights, I listen to at least three more talks. Then later at night I read some of my spiritual books and end off my day with a guided meditation to put me to sleep. I know it is a bit much, but it fills my soul and makes me happy. Plus, I am not harming anyone by enjoying these little pleasures. Be kind to others:

As much as I try, I truly struggle to be a good person. I watched a documentary on the Muslim religion the other night and realised that I am experiencing "Jihad" – an Arabic word which according to Wikipedia means "striving or struggling, especially with a praiseworthy aim".

I find it extremely difficult and nearly impossible to be a good and kind person, yet I want to attain this level of perfection. Be it as it may, it will be my constant companion. I will aim to be a good person even when I am horrible to people until I achieve this status – I have prepared myself for a lifetime achiever award remember.

Forgive yourself and others:

Forgiveness comes at a price – the constant hatred is gone; a huge boulder is lifted and suddenly you can breathe again.

Sometimes hate keeps you warm, I do not know how it works, but it is almost like an achievement to hang on to old hurts and injustices. Where once, resentment, fear, and anger bolstered your ego, you now find peace, love, and forgiveness in its place.

Do you know why you should let it go? Because you deserve better. Hanging on to old pain, fear and loathing is not hurting the other person, it is only slowly but surely killing you. Research shows that hanging on to anger and resentment can cause cancer, so for your own sake, let it go, as it does not serve you any longer. Write down the hurt that was caused and by whom, and then burn the paper – it is gone, now breathe.

Accept good and kindness from others:

If you knew me, you would say, wow that is rich coming from you. Let me tell you something, it is a daily challenge for me to accept kindness, compliments, and help from other people.

I must physically force myself to smile and say thank you and then try to mean it. It is pure agony, but I am getting there. As I said, I am a work in progress.

Research suggests it is a deep-seated belief that you are not worth loving. It hurts me when I hear it as I always thought I had dealt with my childhood pain. But I realise that I am far from it. I am incredibly tenacious though and I will achieve this status one day.

Learn to say no:

This one is harder than it sounds, but again, I am doing remarkably well for a people-pleaser. Learning to say no is the best thing you can do for yourself at any time. If it does not serve your highest good and you will not hurt the person declining, then go ahead and say those dirty words, no thank you! It is liberating and it teaches others to have respect for your time, space, and energy.

Be grateful:

I try to count at least ten things I am grateful for every day, and if I do not have much time, I just make it my usual three. Whatever it is, close your eyes, breathe, taste it, and feel it deeply. It is the most invigorating feeling to be grateful for what you have. Remember the law of attraction - Focus on the good and the positive and those will abound aplenty. Focus on the bad and negative and they will sprout and smother you.

I had to google the twelve steps to recovery from Alcoholics Anonymous (AA) as I never went to any meetings.

These are their steps, which I found similar to the steps I took to heal and recover. I thought "putting yourself first" was one of the steps, but I see it is not listed here. As a recovering addict, you have to put your own needs first – not at the expense of other people, but your sobriety should always, always come first.

If that means, cutting certain friends, family and loved ones out of your life, then you do that. That is one thing I am very strict on, I very rarely surround myself with people who drink, not that I have anything against them, I just know my triggers and I cannot go down that dark and dingy rabbit hole again, ever. So, I come first.

The Alcoholics Anonymous' twelve-step programme:

1. Admit we were powerless over alcohol and that our lives had become unmanageable.
2. Came to believe that a power far greater than ourselves could restore us to sanity.
3. Turned our will and our lives over to the care of God as we understood Him.
4. Made a searching and fearless moral inventory of ourselves.
5. Admitted to God, to ourselves and other human beings, the exact nature of our wrongs.
6. Were entirely ready to have God remove all these defects of character. 7. Humbly asked Him to remove our shortcomings.
7. Made a list of all persons we had harmed and became willing to make amends with them all.
8. Made direct amends with such people, wherever possible, except when to do so would injure them or others.

9. Continued to take personal inventory and when we were wrong promptly admitted it.
10. Sought through prayer and meditation, to improve our conscious contact with God as we understood Him, praying only for knowledge of His will for us and the power to carry that out.
11. Having had a spiritual awakening as the result of these steps, we tried to carry this message to alcoholics and to practice these principles in all our affairs.

I wrote this on my one-year anniversary.

I have a Superpower

This month I get to celebrate an unbelievably beautiful event in my life. One year ago, I decided to stop drinking and smoking for good. It has been one heck of a year. Beautiful and peaceful, but still working through loads of hang-ups, but I am now walking taller, prouder and with crystal clear clarity. So crystal clear that I am starting to think that I have developed a superpower
- lol.
I am not joking. I admit that I am not the most "normal" person out there, but I am not raving mad either. You see, I have developed a superpower where I now see through people.
When I say 'through' people, I do not mean I literally see your intestines; I mean I can see your intentions as clear as I can see my hands in front of me. I used to be a very naïve person, I would believe anything you told me and would only see the good in you. I now struggle to see the good and instead see you for who you truly are. I do not want to sugar-coat it anymore. I do not want to tell white lies to make you feel better anymore.
I sometimes get so angry with myself for not being a better person, for not wanting to be nicer, for refusing to interact with people that I do not like. I have zero tolerance for incompetent, lazy and dishonest people. I have found my voice and I am much better at speaking my mind (perhaps too good at it) now.
On the other hand, I also see myself for who I truly am, and I can tell you something, it is not a pretty sight either. I feel more intensely. When I am happy, I am floating, but when I am upset, I become dark with anger. After the anger, I normally feel a wave of shame and then I get angry all over again for feeling this way.
I have an adverse reaction to 'shamers'; those who try to shame others for being too thin, fat, beautiful, ugly, clever, or dumb. Those who shame others for showing emotions or not conforming to the majority. Yes, it is incredibly tiring having these superpowers.

More times than not, I want to simply pack my bags and go and live in the mountains somewhere far away from people.

When I stopped drinking, I started meditating and found peace and solace in this state of being.

I discovered a deeper connection with the universe, Source, and my angels. I feel pure and good when I am with them; the problem is when I enter the real world with real people, I lose my peace of mind and become a pent-up jack in the box again. Then my finger starts pointing at myself and I try to shame myself for not being perfect.

Good heavens, can you imagine living in this crazy mind of mine?

With all that said and done, I am more content with my life than ever before. I realised that I still have an exceptionally long road ahead of me. I might find many more uphill's and mountains on my path, but at least I will go through it all with eyes wide open.

I am positive that with enough focus and intent, I will one day become good and kind too.

Then perhaps I will see these qualities rare in those around me too. You see; I have been told that I am experiencing enlightenment.

It sounds beautiful right, like Buddha and Jesus, you know, the good guys? So why the heck do I feel like the Incredible Hulk?

Being a journalist at heart, I started researching all of this and found the following quote that makes me feel a little better:

> "Enlightenment is a destructive process.
> It has nothing to do with becoming better or being happier.
> Enlightenment is the crumbling away of untruth.
> It's seeing through the façade of pretence.
> It's the complete eradication of everything we imagined
> to be true."
> – Adyashanti

Would I change anything and want to go back to my old ways? Hell no! Regardless of how grumpy and uncomfortable I feel, at least I know it is real and that somewhere out there, there is a magnitude of angels and Source loving us just the way we are.

So, if you see me on your journey ahead, hide and take the highway to your destination, or else you are more than welcome to join my crazy journey on the gravel road. We might just discover that we are not that bad and create some interesting road signs along the way.

So, I'll see you when I see you, take care.

DAY 19: VULNERABILITY

Today you are letting go of control.

I want you to reach out to someone and ask for their help today.
Accept and trust that the Universe has always got your back. I want you
to try and do something that is not in your control.
For instance, if you always have to cook the food or help the kids with
home- work or drive them to school, then just take one day off and ask
your husband, a friend or family member if they can just help you for
today with that specific task.

Try not to think about it, trust that your aide is doing their best and
they got this. Relax in the knowledge that you don't have to do it all by
yourself and enjoy the free hour or two that this free time is giving you.
It will do you wonders, and I bet you the person you asked will
feel grateful that you trust them enough to ask and accept their
help. Big hug.

Add one thing you are grateful for. Close your eyes and feel the joy.

Positive affirmation: "I am willing and worthy of receiving kindness
in my life."

CHAPTER NINETEEN
THE HOME-INVASION

I told you earlier that we had been wanting to immigrate to another country, any country, so long as it was out of South Africa for over six years.

We wanted to move to the UK in 2013 but we were too young and poor to know how, so we left it and carried on surviving in our country. Until that fateful day, the 10th of August 2018.

It was 2am when I woke up with a flashlight in my eyes. We all think, "If that had to happen to me, I would scream and attack the intruder with anything that I have."

Well, I just froze and could not move. My body broke out in an ice-cold sweat.

I kept my eyes closed shut and gently shook my husband's arm under the blanket, hoping that the intruder could not see what I was doing. My heart was the winner of the F1 race that night and strangely my mind just shut down.

My husband had taken an allergy tablet that evening, so he was fast asleep. Eventually, he woke up and saw the flashlight.

He thought it was just our son sleeping next door and kept saying his name, "James, is that you? James?"

There was no answer and then it finally dawned on him that there was a real threat in our bedroom. We did not know if the intruder had a gun or a knife, if there was more than one person in the house, or if there was someone in the room next door with our boy. Is he alive? Is this person going to kill us? Oh God, the fear was paralyzing until he came charging towards me. The adrenalin was kicking in at a massive speed, and the fear was replaced with anger, "Get out, get out of my house you fucker! Just leave us alone and get out!"

I screamed while kicking him, all the while he carried on running towards me. I then heard the sweet sound "humph" as I kicked him in his soft spots.

I could smell the rancid stink of bushfire on him and the sour stench of stale alcohol crawling off his lips as he exhaled in pain.

Then he grabbed something next to me and he shot out like a bullet into the night from whence he came. It was my phone.

That was it.

All he got for his efforts was my phone, my husband's wallet, jacket, and our housekeys, which was the worst.

Our then three-year-old daughter was sleeping between my husband and I that night (as she would do most nights).

We did not even bother running after him, we ran straight to our son's room to see if he was unharmed. My legs were shaking as I ran to his room, I couldn't even think of the possibility that he could have been harmed. When I saw his big frightened eyes peering from under his blanket, I just cried with relief, "Thank the Lord our family was unharmed."

The trauma we underwent was staggering. We could not sleep.

Not only did we increase the burglar bars on all our windows, but we also changed the locks, added slam lock security gates in front of each door and we installed an extra slam lock at the top of the stairs before you reach our bedrooms.

Plus, we all slept in one bedroom behind a locked door with a chair in front of the door. It was no way to live. We regularly saw a counsellor to talk about our ordeal, but the fear would just not go away.

We eventually sold our property and moved into another house, but the fear remained. Some nights we would set up a shared guarding schedule. I would sleep from 8 pm – 2 am and then wake up and stand guard while it was my husband's turn to sleep.

We were walking zombies and I just could not allow myself to sleep. The doctors refused to give me any more sleeping tablets, so I went from pharmacy to pharmacy buying anti-inflammatory tablets which helped me fall asleep. I overused these tablets and ended up with an ulcer in my stomach. We were a mess, and this was the wake-up call we had been waiting for.

The following month, my husband's brother booked him a ticket to fly to the Netherlands to visit and see if we wanted to live there. After ten days of investigation, my husband returned and said, "We are moving." And that was it.

In December that year, he closed his leather manufacturing business he had been running for ten years. For months prior, his business was just breaking even, and that was without him getting paid a salary.

The economy was slowing down, interest rates were spiking, and the cost of living became even more expensive. I managed to get two great contracts for 2019 and my income was enough to sustain the family, so we decided that my husband would take the year off to recover from the stress of his business and this allowed him to finish his studies to become a personal trainer.

This was something he always had a burning passion for, but never had the time or opportunity to follow through.

In April of that year, we consulted with a lawyer to see what our legal rights were concerning moving.

I still find it hard to explain the shitstorm we faced for wanting to move to a country where the crime was 1% in comparison to ours, unemployment was at 3.3% compared to our 27.7% - just to give our children a better life.

We were following the news religiously regarding the impending Brexit that was due to take place in April 2019.

What were the repercussions going to be for us? When will it happen? By when should we move?

For those of you who do not know about Brexit, it was the withdrawal of the United Kingdom (UK) from the European Union (EU).

The UK held a referendum in June 2016 and the citizens voted to leave the Union. As it stood, the UK was part of the EU, which meant, 'freedom of movement' for all citizens of participating EU states.

If you are a Spanish citizen, you could travel, live and work in any other EU country and vice versa. The EU law also allowed non-EU family members of British citizens to join them in their host country.

That is why we as the non-EU family of a British citizen (my husband) could live and work in the Netherlands, as they are part of the EU state.

In the meantime, our lawyer advised my husband to move to the Netherlands and get a job, a place to stay and prepare for our arrival. To keep our space in the line – so to speak.

I was in tears! We had just experienced a home invasion and now they wanted to split our little family up. It took a lot of convincing but eventually, I agreed. We decided to ask my dad to move in with us while Paul started the processes overseas.

So, in September, Paul and I flew to the Netherlands to scout for options and I instantly fell in love. The people are so incredibly friendly and helpful, the skies are as beautiful and blue as ours. There are beaches, and the language is quite like my home language, Afrikaans.

Because my husband is a British citizen, he could come and go as he pleased, but we needed visas, so we set up an appointment with the International Naturalisation Department (IND) for October and off I went, back to SA leaving my husband behind to start the processes from there.

In between all of this, I had been creating vision boards, meditating intently, and focusing everything I had on immigrating successfully. I even fasted for four days and four nights.

I did not allow myself to eat anything. I just drank fluids and prayed. I try to fast three times a year, to cleanse my body and mind, and to connect with God and my Angels on a higher frequency.

During one of these fasts, I became so bitterly sad when I realised how painful and empty life feels without food to be enjoyed.

A simple luxury we take for granted every day.

To live without food felt empty and pointless and I thought, "This is what it must feel like for people starving, who have no food to eat, not because of choice, but because there is no money to buy any." Imagine the turmoil, pain, and suffering millions of people go through every day. As a mother, I could not bear seeing my child suffer. This is not right. We need to do more to spread the love and our resources. No one should have to go hungry at night.

I recently had one of my old contacts ask me for money as they were starving. I sent him money and advised him to try The Law of Attraction. I advised him to focus on the good and stop reading the news, to feel lucky and blessed, and write down his vision and wishes for the future. He said he would, and I did not hear from him again. About one month later, he asked for money again and I said, "I cannot always help you with cash as this is something you need to do for yourself. Are you writing your wishes down?

Do you believe that you are worthy of receiving?"

He needed to feel the excitement of landing that dream job and having pockets full of cash. He said he understood and would do so. Another month went by and he said, "I am so sorry to ask you again, but we are really struggling. I asked him again, "Have you been writing your dreams down?

Are you putting in the work to manifest your desires?" He said, yes. Another donation from a kind gentleman was made to his account and the next day, he texted me to say he had a job interview the following week. We celebrated the news and I said to him, "It is done, this one is yours, claim it, make it yours. Get your work clothes out, shine those shoes, and start setting your alarm to get up early as if you are starting work already."

The following week he came back to me and said, "I got the job!" That simple. I felt that I had to include this as I am a firm believer in The Law of Attraction and since I became sober, I have been using this newfound power to my advantage and things always work out for me. In October that year, I only had one contract left, as the other one had already expired. We then received the news that the house we were renting, was being sold and our contract was ending in November. The kids were missing their father, we had no place to stay or income from the end of that November and our lawyer would not go any further with our case. But I felt that the time was right, that we needed to make the move before Brexit was implemented and before getting too old to adapt and start a new life. I always had a thing that you must know where you are going in life when you reach forty.

Well two months later, our home and contents were sold, I had a buyer for my business, visas, and plane tickets for the kids, and off we went to Cape Town for a "holiday."

I only told a select few people that we were leaving in December.

DAY 20: GO WITHIN

Cut out all social media, news, and WhatsApp messages for one day.

You will be amazed how much negativity the constant feeding of information creates in your subconscious mind.
If you must watch a movie today, do not watch anything containing violence or aggression.
Declutter your mind and if you have a chance, clean your house.
You will feel as light as a feather after a good spring clean.
Clutter and dirt have an extremely negative effect on us, and we do not notice until it is all gone.
List what you have done today.

Add one thing you are grateful for. Close your eyes and feel the joy.

Positive affirmation: "My mind is free; thus, I am free."

CHAPTER TWENTY
SOCIAL MEDIA (2019)

Since we left Cape Town in December 2019, I did not post on social media for over six months. In this regard, I am a proper crab (Cancer – moon baby).

When I am scared and uncertain, I retract and go within myself. So, I went off all social media channels - Facebook, Instagram, LinkedIn, WhatsApp, and E- mail - for a full month!

In principle it sounds easy to just unplug for a while, but by my insanity, it was hard.

I did not realise how addicted I was to these tools until I could not use them anymore.

I would get irritable and scratchy and restless and did not know what to do with myself. I drove myself nuts. I cleaned my house, then cleaned it again, and then just a little more cleaning and renovating. I baked, read, and watched movies, and then as soon as I sat down and did nothing, I would get itchy again. That incessant desire to keep looking at what is happening out there, to see if anyone posted on one of my old comments, if anyone posted anything interesting that I may be missing out on. Wondering how 'so and so' was doing, and whether I should just check in quickly and see... It was a constant itch that I just could not scratch aka addiction.

I recently watched, 'The Social Dilemma' and it scared me to death. I have always been a bit averse to technology, but this explained how it affects us perfectly.

This is exactly what I went through, and I still find myself constantly checking all my apps. I realised that I check almost every 15 - 30 minutes to see if I have any new notifications.

I start with WhatsApp, then Facebook which keeps me there for nearly five minutes, just scrolling like a baboon. I manage to tear myself off and check Instagram, then I check all my business pages, then I check my emails, and then just before I get back to work I check google to see if there is any new interesting information for me.

So, a quick little check turns out to be nearly ten minutes at a time and this is quick folks. This can easily turn into four to seven hours a day by just "quickly checking my notifications" ... A day, people!

The seriousness of overuse of social media was being studied by Dar Meshi, lead author and assistant professor at MSU.

The findings, published in the Journal of Behaviour Addictions, are the first to examine the relationship between social media use and risky decision- making capabilities.

"With so many people around the world using social media, we must understand its use," Meshi said.

"I believe that social media has tremendous benefits for individuals, but there's also a dark side when people can't pull themselves away. We need to better understand this drive so we can determine if excessive social media use should be considered an addiction."

This is scary, I do not know if you think this is ok, because it is not. It is dumbing us down and keeping us hooked on our devices and what is making it even worse is the feeds it "feeds" you.

It is feeding us our latent addiction. For instance, if you google fitness and food often, then it will push feeds that relate to these topics and this is when it gets scary.

It steers you to watch controversial stories about these topics and before you know it, you have joined "Get Fat" groups shaming thin and happy people and fake news channels push their propaganda to divide and inspire hate in you even more.

What scares me the most (and there is a lot to be scared about), is the fact that we so passionately believe in our 'truth'.

What the algorithm of social media is designed to do, is track and study your behaviour to such a degree, that it knows when you are happy, sad, hungry, your tastes, your favourite colour, your personality type, your beliefs and what you feel neutral about.

Now that the social media channels know you better than you know yourself, they push information on your 'feed' so that you see more of those posts.

Advertisers pay these social media channels a large sum of money to push their products in front of you so that you buy their products. That is still kind of ok for me, but what is unacceptable for me, is manipulating me in such a manner that I start changing my perception and even beliefs of what is going on around me.

Take Covid-19 for example.

Now, this is getting big people, so bear with me.

I am an addict.

Fine, I accept that. But they know that I have an addictive personality and they also know that I believe in alternative healing and treatments, meditations, etc. because they can see my searched topics on the internet. They know according to my personality type that I am open to alternative theories or what you call conspiracy theories. So, what do they push in my feed? A lot of conspiracy theories, that I fervently believed in.

Please note the "d" after 'believe'. After watching The Social Dilemma, I am even starting to doubt these theories and am now doubting everything.

What is the truth? How am I going to find the truth? How am I going to really know what is true and what is false?

We are slowly but surely being programmed to hate each other more. Think back to when you were younger, and you held different opinions to your friends. You would bicker, laugh, and perhaps shout at each other, but the next day, you would have a good chuckle at each other's crazy theories and move on.

But not today. What is the matter with society? When did we become so self-entitled and small-minded?

(Please note I am including myself here, as I also fell victim to this willing form of slavery).

Today, if your opinion differs from another, you simply unfriend them on social media and stop taking their calls.

Why? Because they dared to have an opinion different from yours. They are wrong, you are right and that is that.

Unfortunately, this does not prove that you are passionate about your beliefs, it only proves that you are a bigot and ignorant.

(Please note I am including myself here again too.)

Seriously people, as a collective, we must let go of this belief that we are right and anyone else that thinks differently from us is wrong and means they are bad people.

You are not bad just because you think differently, you are merely being a human being that exercises your right to freedom of speech and thoughts. We need to become more tolerable of others, regardless of their race, age, sex, beliefs, and political support.

We are destroying the fundamental link that makes us human - our compassion and love for each other.

Is it that important to always be right?

Does it take away your individualism if you accept others that are different from you?

Does it mean you are not a strong woman if you enjoy the company of men and being treated with softness and love?

Does it really mean that you are not a man if you feel sad and sometimes feel the need to cry? No! It is utter nonsense!
Please, for the wellbeing of society and the future of your children, we must learn to accept others for who they are and love them anyway.

My husband and I recently had a long discussion about this topic. We had watched the movie two nights before and watched it again with our children the next day. It honestly shook me to my core.
It is unravelling all the fervent beliefs I so passionately believed in.
I am scared and uncertain of myself, the world, society, my beliefs, and everything I hold dear.
My husband is a big geek and has been a big fan of superheroes since he was a little boy. To the extent that when he was about eight years old, he was teased and poked at because he played with the action figures, He-Man, and Thundercat's.
In South Africa in the eighties, things were very conventional, and the religious leaders believed that all imaginary heroes were straight from Satan and so my husband was labelled a satanic worshipper and the kids destroyed his action heroes.
Today, he is still a big child when it comes to superheroes, but he is starting to feel disenfranchised when he sees how they are politically correcting his childhood heroes. He feels like he is being forced to feel ashamed of his heritage (as a white male bornin the eighties).
Politically Correct i.e. the fear of saying something that will offend the minority.
I do not even know where to begin because my heart is so sore as I write this. What have we become and how did we get here?
How is it ok for a woman to say, "all men are trash" or for a person of colour to say, "only white people are racists" or for an obese person to say, "skinny people are judgmental"?
I personally know four bad men out of the thousands of men I know.
I do not want my beautiful boy to grow up with the label, "all men are trash". He is not trash, and neither is my husband, my father and in fact most of the men I know, are not trash.
How is it ok for people to say only their opinion matters?
What about my opinion, and those of my husband, son or father, and millions of others that are being affected by these kinds of statements?
Just because you have been disenfranchised for years, does not make it ok to turn the tide on those that have been your oppressor for years.
That is called revenge.

I am not saying what happened to you in the past is ok. I am part of the minority. In South Africa, being white is the minority.

Plus, being female is yet another minority.
Do I stand on every corner or chat group shouting, "I am white, I am woman, my opinion matters not yours!"
No! Because that would be ignorant, childish, and self-entitled.

We need to learn to love more and hate less, give more, and want less. The thing is most young people or Millennials (me included) and Generation Z's today, have been brought up by the internet and all things social. They/we can do things, that very few Generation X and Baby Boomers can do.
Unfortunately, most of the youth of today only had one form of "truth" growing up – the internet.
They have been brought up to believe that what the internet tells them is the truth, whereas we had our parents, their friends, people in authority, and of course books as our source of information and "truth".
Some of the differences I have noticed between the age groups is that we (aka the older generation), are a lot happier and more confident, while today's youth, and as a race, have become rather angry. We used to be confident and happy growing up.
We were taught from a young age to just get things done. You were shown once how to do something, and then you just had to wing it. Growing up, we had to compete with the prettiest or most handsome kid in our school or neighbourhood.
That was it.
If we went out partying all night and got horribly drunk, there was no evidence except for someone that might have seen you do it and hopefully, they were just as drunk as you and forgot by the next morning. We did not set out to go out and have a good night and see how many people we could catch in the act of doing something stupid or embarrassing.
We were therefore happier as we did not have the stresses of what people on social media would think of us, being exposed to such a large audience – instantaneously. It would scare me to death if I had to deal with all those comments and judgements.

Today's youth have it a lot worse than we did. Yes, we were brought up harder in a way, we had more hidings, beatings, and severe punishments, but we did not have such high expectations to live up to as the youth do nowadays
- thanks to social media.

We had more will power and endurance. If we had a school project, we had to do research in libraries and interview people who were experts in their fields. It used to take us weeks.

Today, you simply google things in a couple of minutes.

I wonder if the youth even know what the inside of a library looks like. It is big and beautiful, filled with the most amazing array of books.

Looking up a topic about a historical person, for instance let's say Thomas Edison, would mean going to the library, and then if you were brave enough, you would ask the librarian which section you could search for Edison.

She might be kind enough to take you to that section, where you would have to sift through about one-hundred-and-twenty books to find Edison, or she would just wave you into the vague area where the book might be found. By the end of the day, you had hopefully found four books containing information about him, and then you had to book them out to take home to read. From this information, you would make notes and hopefully in three to four weeks, have enough information to submit your project.

One thing is for sure though, you ended up knowing that person better than you know yourself.

Today, with the ease of the internet, you only retain the information for as long as you need to and then you forget it, and this is why I find the older generation have a lot more willpower and endurance, and even work ethics. We were a lot more independent and creative than today's youngsters too because we did not have social media and devices to keep us entertained all day long. We just had to make things up as they came along. We did not have all the answers and our parents sure as heck did not know everything either. We had to figure things out and just hope for the best. If something was broken, we had to find a way to fix it.

'MacGyver' was our go-to guy. He could fix an airplane with a wire and a rope
– I am not kidding!

If MacGyver could do it, then surely, we could do it too. I often tell my children to just unplug and allow themselves to do nothing for a while. Not playing with toys, watching movies, or anything, just to be.

Yes, they get irritated and bored, but they do come up with great ideas because that is when inspiration hits – when your mind is no longer cluttered and is free to think up innovative ways to play or create.

We respected our parents, or anyone older than us, especially our teachers. We would be naughty and get punished with a hiding and we would take it. We accepted that our actions had consequences and we never backchatted our parents or teachers.

It was unheard of for a child to interrupt an adult, otherwise you would get the biggest hiding of your life later that night.
Oh, and we never complained to our parents about how "horrible" a teacher was to us, ever!
That would give you one thing and one thing only, "What did you do to deserve that?
If I find out you are misbehaving at school, you will get it!"
We were brought up a little more conservative, maybe only in South Africa. We were disciplined and punished when wrong, but we were also given more freedom to move around.
We were not babied. Today, we baby our children. My boy fell off his bicycle and split his lip, knocked his tooth back, and got a brace for it.
We were told to get him a helmet with a faceguard in the front.
Can you imagine wearing that thing as a child? You would have received such a beating, or worse, shunned from society, no-one would want to play with you anymore, because you looked stupid. (Even though I now bought him one and he kind of look cool in it.)
We also had a lot more freedom. We could go out anytime and play with our friends, our parents did not care where we were, so long as we were back home for dinner.
Now we need to put trackers on our children, and they must check in with us every hour to make sure they are still alive. I did not hear from my boy for two hours when he went out playing with his friends in the park. I could not reach him on his phone, so I jumped in the car and started driving around the village until I found him. Yes, I have became that parent...
We were truthful. That is what has hit me the hardest. How the truth has been manipulated and how we react to it.
As I said earlier, the youth of today were brought up by the internet and social media. You learned from a young age, that the way you look is imperfect.
There are thousands of apps available to 'beautify' us, which must mean we are not perfect the way we are.
This interestingly, is also why men are generally more confident than women. They were not taught from a young age to wear make-up and colour their hair to make them look more attractive.
They could just shave, shower and off they went – looking just fabulous thank you very much.
But not girls, no, girls have to wear some blush and a little lip-gloss and mascara to make their eyes pop and add some colour to make their eyes pop a little bit more, and your bum must be kind of big, but not too big, and the list goes on and on. That is a young girl's truth.
But I digress.

My point has almost been established.
If you have read this far, you will know that the algorithms on social media track you and know you better than you know yourself.
You have been 'fed' a certain 'truth' for as long as you have been on social media, which for most people now is from the age of nine or ten years of age. Your truth has therefore been skewed. It has led you down a path to influence your thoughts and beliefs and manipulated you to believe a certain 'fact' as truth.

This is what my husband and I were arguing about this morning.
He was angry at one of the Social Justice Warriors who said something on Instagram, and I suggested that perhaps he should feel sorry for them.
Perhaps they too are simply victims of being misled and manipulated to think in a certain manner.
It is easier to let other people think for you and to let them tell you what to do, than to try and work it out for yourself.

What I am trying to say is, perhaps they have all been force-fed a certain way of thinking as the God's truth and nothing and no one can persuade them that they are wrong.

I thought back to when I was in my twenties and I was all bright-eyed and bushy-tailed and believed that politicians were there to make a difference. I believed that they had been solemnly sworn in to protect us and do what is right for us as a collective.
But this is so far from the truth, they are there to serve their parties and reap the money and bend reality to their will, as they see fit, regardless if it is for the greatest good of mankind. You would not have been able to persuade me that my beliefs are wrong. How more so can we persuade the youth that what they perceive as the ultimate truth is perhaps not the absolute truth. That they have been manipulated like puppets on a string to think a certain way.
How does that make you feel?

Ok, I went off on a full rant there and I still feel that I am nowhere near to expressing my thoughts and feelings about it, but I will leave it at that for now. Please just think about it ok. It is important.

So back to when I went off social media. After a month had passed, I became what is known as a 'lurker'. I would just read everyone's posts and see what they were up to and find out what the latest news and trends were. It felt good not to post anything. Sometimes it is good to just take a break from all outside interferences and just concentrate on healing yourself first. Some find healing in sharing their feelings while others show aggression and join action groups.

Whatever works for you, is great. We are all different and I respect that. I have, however, learned a few things from just observing my contacts posts and reading people's reactions to life.

As a human race, we are way more connected than we originally thought. Throw in one common enemy or thing to fight for and people from all races, ages, sexes, and creeds will band together and connect. It is amazing really.

I enjoyed watching how people would band together against the government in SA during lockdown - how dare they tell us that we cannot drink and smoke or buy bathmats and only go out for three hours in the morning. I know how bad alcohol and cigarettes are, but that still does not give them the right to tell us how to live our lives. You, however, did not just lie down and accept it, you fought back – tooth and nail. I loved seeing how everyone rallied together and found solace in each other's stories and shared frustration.

Everybody simply wants to be heard. It does not matter how small or big their frustration, anger or joy is, social media allowed us to share our thoughts and feelings – in the hopes of being heard and to be understood. (You see I am not against social media; I love it and use it daily. But it should never be your ruler or teacher or sole source of knowledge and information – it is about balance.)

You also like being told what to do, for a while. Most people thoroughly enjoyed the lockdown, but only for the first three weeks, and then it became too much. That is the average holiday time we take a year – three weeks. Go figure.

You are not stupid.

I was pleasantly surprised by how you questioned everything after a while. You would look at "conspiracy theories" and give them due consideration. I believe you must keep an open mind. Doubt everything, ask questions, and never just accept what "they", say as the truth.

You are also mostly kind. You took the time to see how you could help those less fortunate than you.

You rallied up funding for those who had no food, found ways to deliver the food to them – knowing that you could have been arrested.

Do not forget how kind everyone has been, the world needs to become kinder and more considerate to those in need.

You are so brave. I have been in utter awe of how you all took the radical changes in your stride.

The hardships, the fear, the anxiety, and sometimes despair.

You kept your sense of humour regardless of how dire your situation seemed. I love that South Africans especially, have the best sense of humour. We endure so much in our country that we find solace and familiarity in our humour, even if it is at one's own expense.

You are highly creative too. My goodness, I have seen such innovative ways of people earning money online and via social media and it gladdened my heart.

Some artists would perform live and you could donate to their accounts. I loved how you found new creative ways of making money - sewing masks and breweries changing to create ventilation machines, it is amazing.

Those that are angry at the world and themselves, will find innovative ways to hurt those around them. From spying on their neighbours to see if they were keeping within the lockdown rules, to informing the police of these transgressions, to sharing stories of hate and pain.

I have learned that you cannot heal those that do not want to be healed. Just avoid them and don't give in to your anger.

**"If you don't like where you are – move.
You are not a tree!" – Jim Rohn**

DAY 21: GRATITUDE

Today I want you to make a list of everything you are grateful for in your life.

In the beginning it takes a while to get into. But as you progress, you find that it just flows.
Start small by giving thanks for a roof over your head, a warm bed to sleep in, food in your fridge, the beautiful flowers, or
birds outside your window, and then move on to your eyesight, your hearing, your strong heartbeat, your loved ones and most importantly – give thanks for being you! Enjoy the process.

Close your eyes and feel the gratitude for all your blessings, small and big.

Positive affirmation: "I am grateful for my life. I love myself and I love my life. I create my own reality. Thank you."

CHAPTER TWENTY-ONE
ARRIVING IN THE
NETHERLANDS (2019 - 2020)

Not only did I escape what I perceived was my tormentor, but also
my country, which has been torn apart by corruption, violence,
and poverty.
A country I still love and ache for every day.
I miss the warmth of the sun breathing down on me, the smell of sea
mixed with sweat and smoke, and I miss the shouting and beeping of
the taxis that are ready to take you out in a second.
But mostly, I miss my friends and family, and the familiarity of small
things I would normally take for granted, like my favourite brand and
knowing in which aisle the porridge was.
It is small things, but I miss it.
I built up a beautiful network for myself over the last few years and I
earned respect from my peers.
It was hard work to achieve that level of status, and now I need to start
the process all over again.

I was 39 years old, had two degrees behind me, started eight
businesses, won four awards, and there were many opportunities to
make money in my country, but I had to leave it all behind and become
a cleaner in the Netherlands. It was not an easy decision and I had
my doubts, but I knew I had to do it for my children. Their safety and
security are the only things that matter to me.
You see, I am many things. I am not a particularly good person, I am
mean and spiteful, I am vengeful and quick to anger, but by God, the
only thing I am truly proud of is being a mother.
There is nothing and I mean nothing in this world I will not do for
them. I will lie, steal, and even kill to keep them safe and happy.
I will break those damn rules to ensure their safety and security.

Before arriving in The Netherlands with the children in December, I had to go back in October for my interview with the IND (for my working visa).

My husband had just started work, so he could not meet me at the airport, and we agreed that I would go to our hotel and wait for him there until he finished work.

We had to be in Amsterdam the following day for my working visa and were assured that if we applied before Brexit, and my husband has a job, we can all live and work in the Netherlands.

Easy...

So, I arrived at Schiphol airport at about 11 am that morning, and after checking out it was the afternoon. I had a huge travel bag on wheels with me, as well as another bag I was carrying over my shoulder and a rucksack too. I thought I could manage all of this easily as the one bag was on wheels. At the airport, I planned my trip to my accommodation. It seemed easy, catch one train to Amstel, cross the bridge and 200m on I would be there.

Well... Those 200m turned in 4km, the wheels on my travel bag eventually broke off and I was in a state.

There I was in a strange country, dragging over 40kg of luggage around. I had no internet and no airtime to phone anyone.

I just could not find the place and walked aimlessly around the block three times, I even had locals helping me find the street.

I was so tired, it was raining, I was wearing only a string top, my face was blood red from the strain, and I was crying with frustration.

I then saw a business place that for some reason looked inviting, so I left my luggage outside on their steps and asked the gentleman behind the counter to please phone my hotel and call a porter.

"Excuse me, sorry, I am a bit lost. I have been looking for my hotel for over an hour now, my bag just broke and I cannot move it any further. Can you please dial this number and ask the hotel to send a porter to come and help me with my luggage?"

Yes. I said my porter must come and fetch my luggage from these premises. For those of you who don't know what a porter is; it is that lovely man dressed in a uniform that meets you at front door of your larger hotels, such as Hilton or Radisson Blu and who carries your luggage to your room.

He just looked at me like I was insane. He kept saying, "Please take a seat mam, have some water."

I was oblivious to all of this.

I just kept asking him if he could please just phone the hotel for my porter to come and help me.

Well, he did not, because he was not allowed to phone, and I think he silently thought I was a bit 'special' in the head.

He did help me google the place though and it was just 200m away, so, I took a deep breath, threw my bags over my shoulder, and dragged my 40kg of luggage behind me. It made the most terrible noise on the cobblestone streets. A granny was walking in front of me with her grandson, and she was literally dragging him behind her as he was walking backwards staring at me. I must have looked like an alien from outer space.

Eventually, I reached my destination, and I was so relieved until I saw the inside...

To me, it looked more like a brothel than anything else. There were no "porters" available, and that is when I realised that we could not simply "wing" it anymore.

We were in a strange country, we speak a different language, our customs are different, and that was our new normal.

I was so excited to see my husband that week, it was his birthday and our anniversary, and I received my visa - there was so much to celebrate. During this visit, I also met the most amazing person, Carol. The village we lived in was beautiful, like a fairy-tale.

I went for loads of walks and during one of them, I stumbled across a company of interest to me.

I thought, how interesting, let me connect with the owner and see if she has any advice for me regarding work.

I sent her a message on Facebook, and she agreed to meet with me.

We enjoyed a delicious cup of hot chocolate together and instantly connected (it was a friend at first sight kind of thing).

It is rare to make new friends so late in our lives.

Life is consumed with work and family, and a lot of people do not believe in making friends with people at work.

Carol is funny, smart, kind, and crazy – she ticked all the boxes and I blossomed in her presence.

She adopted our little family from the get-go.

Her beautiful family took us under their wing and made us feel like we belonged.

They gave us furniture from their homes, fed us, took us sightseeing, and loved us as if we were family.

I cannot stress enough how these seemingly insignificant, small acts of kindness saved my life.

They made me feel alive again, dragged me out of the deepest pit of despair, and thawed the fear and anxiety with their care and love. They made me feel like I was worth something again. It is unbelievable how quickly you forget the life before the one you have now. I will forever be grateful for this beautiful friendship.

Paul and I left for The Netherlands on the 11th of September, for him to set up our life and for me to get a mental picture of what to expect. My first impression was dreamy. I felt so safe there that I cried the first night I arrived. I instantly loved it.

Everything was so pretty, the houses, the gardens, the parks, the streets, everything. The people were friendly and helpful, and the weather was pleasant. My first weekend in Medemblik I was lucky enough to experience the annual Horseracing event. The entire town was kitted out in theme, the main street was blocked off for the racing, the kids were given off from school and there were activities on every street corner. They had a mini carnival for the kids at the back, a mini "Amazing Race," three streets down, and a beer and entertainment tent at the entrance of the town. I was gobsmacked.

I could not believe so much could take place in such a small town.

Let me tell you something, Medemblik is truly one of the hidden gems of the Netherlands. It is a yachting village, rich in history, and has a beautiful castle at the mouth of the ocean (which is not sea salt because of the Dijk).

I became so excited and could not wait to bring the children over to experience all this beauty.

We registered the children with ease in the local school that also provided a Dutch class where the children first learnt to speak Dutch, before proceeding to the grades they were meant to be in.

I must say, I do not think there is a country in the world that looks after its citizens as well as the Dutch. They are truly amazing when it comes to caring for their citizens. Each child receives an average of 250 Euros every term which their parents can use for their children's clothing, transport or treats. Schooling and health care are free for all children. If you earn a minimum salary every month, they also give you extra money towards your child's transport, and even money towards extra curriculum activities such as dancing or swimming lessons.

They even provide you with a bicycle, laptop, and printer if you do not have one. It is crazy.

Everything is set up to help you with your children.

They pay a portion towards care for your babies before they go to school, although they encourage mothers to stay at home until the child is five years old and ready for school. If you earn minimum wage, you also get subsidies on your rental and health insurance.

It is also very normal for you to only work three days a week.

On a minimum wage salary, you should earn 950 Euros a month, which will cover your expenses if your rent is 400 Euros.

For locals, this is a normal rental cost. Your food will cost you about 60 Euros per week for a family of four people, so the cost of living is relatively good.

Your health Insurance is 100 Euros a month, so as you can see you can easily survive on a three-days a week salary.

But we were not so lucky.

We paid 1400 Euros a month for our rent. It did include, electricity, gas, and Wi-Fi, but it was still insanely expensive. We could not find another place to rent for less than 1000 Euros a month anywhere in the Netherlands. There is a huge demand for houses and apartments. They have a strict law when it comes to building and, in the end, it costs the builder too much money to build new houses.

On the one hand, more and more people are entering the country and on the other hand, you have a limited number of new houses being built, so it becomes severely imbalanced.

I tried to find jobs in Amsterdam (which is much more cosmopolitan and has English jobs available), but they want you to live in Amsterdam to work there. So, for me to get a job I had to move to Amsterdam, pay a rental of 1400 Euros and then hope to get a job very soon to start affording the rent.

I doubt there is a country more officious than the Netherlands.

Everything is recorded. You need to report to your local municipality if you move into a new village, even if you are just on holiday. They want to know every single thing about you, where you are from, who you are married to, what you are doing in their country, where your children go to school and if you are registered for tax. You must register on what they call 'Digi D' and remember, everything is in Dutch. If it wasn't for my Afrikaans background, I would not have been able to get by. I do not know how foreigners who do not understand the language survive.

There is a helpline you can call, and they can converse in English with you, but for some reason, they took great offence every time they heard my surname and realised I could not speak Dutch.

They would get so annoyed and ask me numerous times, "How can you not speak Dutch with a surname such as yours."

I got so fed up that in the end I just said, "Well in 1680 the Dutch arrived in South Africa, started a colony, and then left us there". She was so shocked she just put me through to the next person to try and help me. Apparently, my husband's surname is almost like royalty there – go figure. In all honesty, I think my expectations were too high.

I thought I would integrate relatively easily as I can understand them perfectly well, I just cannot speak Dutch, although they can understand me if I speak a little bit of Afrikaans.

They found it very "grappig" (funny). I think I felt like I was coming back to my roots, and because The Netherlands is where my forefathers are from, I thought I would be treated as such.

Perhaps if we lived in one of the bigger cities, things would have been different, I do not know.

I started a business in those few months too - offering entrepreneurial workshops to school children and then Covid-19 struck. I hated the fact that I could not get any proper work and that I was only good for manual work. It sucked the life-force out of me.

I lost nearly 10kg in the five months that we were there. That is what unhappiness does to me.

If it were not for my sweet, beautiful friend who kept encouraging us and trying to include us in their warm, loving lives, I cannot say what would have become of me and my family.

In the end, the Netherlands was our haven. It was relatively easy for us to live and work in and provided us with a surprising route into Scotland. For that, I will forever be thankful for the country and giving us refuge while away from South Africa – so,

"Dank je wel, Holland!" (Thank you very much Netherlands!)

CHAPTER TWENTY-TWO
THE THING ABOUT A
PASSPORT

All this moving had me thinking long and hard about this seemingly insignificant thing called a Passport.

Sometimes I feel powerless, like I have no state – no rights. I feel like I do not belong anywhere.

South Africa is no longer my home and cannot provide for my family. The Netherlands is no longer my home either and here I am now in the United Kingdom, not yet feeling accepted.

I have no British passport or residency card to protect my status here. I am, pending...

Most of the time I am honestly fine with that. My job keeps me busy and I have so much to be grateful for that it does not affect me too much, but now and again I just think, what if I had a different passport.

So where does this passport thing come from?

It all started during the First World War and was created by the League of Nations. You are shit out of luck if you were born in a poor country from there on out, but if you were born in a first-world country, well then you are fine, your country will be protected.

Listen, I get it. I understand that you have to have some form of control over of who comes in and out of your country, but it does not sit well with me that we cannot simply jump on a plane or ship and travel to a far off land, see if we like it and then move there. Why not?

If we can contribute to the economy and we are a good citizen, then why can we not be offered this opportunity to better our lives?

Because I was born in Namibia, I could claim a Namibian passport. But as I was brought up in South Africa, I now have a South African passport. My husband has a British passport (as I said before), our kids have South African passports and I now have a Dutch Residency Card.

Let me tell you something, I am way better off than most people who only have their South African passports and are simply stuck there. That is their lot in life forever. In South Africa, we have the leader of the EFF, Julius Malema, screaming for white people's blood – "Go back to your bloody country you Colonials," he shouts.

Guess what Malema, most of them are trying to leave the country and leave you to rot, but other countries do not wish to take us in, because of this new passport control, slash, immigration control law that some men sixty years ago decided we all need from here on out.

They fear overcrowding or some other reason. Luckily for them, before the first world war, they could go to any country, take control of it, take their minerals and assets, and then leave it to rot. Then take that wealth back to their countries and not even blink an eye when you ask them for a chance to live in their countries – cause you see, now we have passports and we have to get permission to get into a country...

So, my children and I are currently stateless. We don't belong anywhere and sometimes I feel like an alien here, not as much as I did before, but enough to wish the kids and I could just get the same passport as my husband and that I can also feel like I belong somewhere. The worse is the wait.

Your fate, your life, your existence is at the hands of someone sitting in their office and looking through your documents, deciding then and there if you can live in the country or not. It literally depends on one person, how that person feels on that morning, his or her level of knowledge and experience, his or her level of compassion and understanding and then your fate is dealt.

I phoned the Home Office about twenty times since I started the processes in March. Guess what?

Every single time I phone, I get a new answer.

The one says, "You can work", then next one says, "No you can't work". Then the next one says, "Of course you can work", then the next one says, "No you cannot work". It is a nightmare!

I always said, people that work in governmental grants departments or small business development must come with a resume of being previously self- employed first.

The same should apply to people working in Home Office. They should either be a foreigner or have a family member that is from another country.

They need to be able to make an informed decision and done in a compassionate manner.

Sometimes it is nice to be boxed in – being classified (in a good way you know.)

What did I say about those damn rules...? Ooh yes – Break them!

I sometimes wish I could just sit here, light my candle, wish for a British passport, and the next morning wake up and there it is – all pretty and maroon just like my favourite bottle of Merlot.
I do not know why not.
I think I am worthy; I think I have been a good girl and I think I deserve one.
Shouldn't that qualify as a good enough reason for me to get one?

CHAPTER TWENTY-THREE
COVID -19

Let us go back a few months...
I simply cannot write this book and not include the global pandemic that crippled the world.
I remember sitting in my friend's lounge in Medemblik talking and laughing at how serious people are taking Covid-19 and how ridiculous it all is.
Well, one month later, I was unable to work as we had all fallen ill. It was so bad. I felt like I had constant panic attacks, I could not breathe, and my chest was so tight.
I phoned the doctor and she asked if my temperature was still high, I said no. She replied that there was nothing they could do for me; I just needed to take Paracetamol and will be better in no time.
I explained to her that I could not breathe, and she said it was a panic attack due to the stress I was under.
I was like, "Girl, please, I come from South Africa, I don't get panic attacks because of a silly virus", so she said she would ask a phycologist to phone me and talk me through my stress.
I was livid, to say the least.
Anyhow, a week later, I had recovered except for the stomach inflammation that persisted for months as they refused to give me antibiotics.
It was a crazy time to be alive.
In the Netherlands, we had been in intelligent lockdown from the 13th of March. Schools and public events closed, and then the restaurants and service industries that were in close contact with people also closed. We were advised to stay indoors and only go outside if we had to. From what I saw, everyone was still out on the streets, some restaurants were still open, clothing stores were open, and yes you could not find toilet paper, pasta, and flour for nearly two weeks. People did however stay 1.5 meters away from the person next to them, but nothing else major changed.

By the 22nd of April, the death toll was 3916 of which 34134 people tested positive.

I would not read anything into the confirmed cases as only the severely ill and hospitalized people were tested for the virus, so the real figure should be about 500000 people that were infected. As a matter of interest, I am also including the UK, as that is where we are heading next. 129044 infected and 17337 deaths, which is dark. In South Africa, there were only 3465 infected and 58 deaths at the time.

In the Netherlands, they were very relaxed about it, but the UK took severe steps, and the country was in full lockdown, as well as South Africa. The difference here is that the Netherlands and UK are first-world countries that could look after their citizens and businesses, ensuring that they received funding from the government to sustain themselves. South Africa is not in that position and people hardly received a few hundred Rands to buy food for the month.

The people were already starving before the virus but could at least go and sell their wares on the street corner to feed their family for one evening.

Unfortunately, if you are under full lockdown then no one will be able to buy your goods and your family will starve.

They brought out even more ridiculous rules that said no one could hand out food parcels to the poor without the government's approval. They cannot even run their own departments, never mind the country, how are they going to feed millions of people?

They had the army patrolling the streets and made sure no one was buying cigarettes or alcohol but would not use those same people to hand out food parcels to the poor. I thank sweet Jesus that we escaped while we still could. When we arrived in the UK, they were still under lockdown, but people could go out for exercise and they started easing the restrictions a bit. The Netherlands was almost back to normal, schools were open, restaurants were in operation and people were back at work. We heard so many different rumours, that we might have to self-isolate for two weeks when arriving in the UK, and that we were not allowed to travel too far away from home, but they were not that strict. Many theories went around during this time.

The first one said Covid-19 was created in a lab in China with the backing of the American Government. China released the virus into America to fight them in this way.

The second one said it was 5G and not the virus that was causing the symptoms that people were experiencing – similar symptoms to being poisoned.

The third one was also that it was created and designed to be released to create panic amongst the public who will turn to their government for answers and help. The government will then keep them in fear and release the vaccine that contains the deadly MERS virus that will kill the weak or leave you sterile. There was also another one that said the vaccine will contain a chip so the government can track your every move. I do not know which one to believe, but as my husband says, "The truth is somewhere in between."

I believe that our bodies are designed to fight off any illness that comes their way. Our bodies are simply reactors to our emotions. That is the key, if we believe that we are healthy and envision ourselves as happy, healthy, and powerful human beings, able to do whatever we put our minds to, then it shall be so.

If on the other hand, we believe that we have weak immune systems, and the virus will kill us, chances are extremely high that this is exactly what will happen. Whatever you believe – it will be so.

Unfortunately, what the world leaders as a collective have done is strip the individual of their most basic human right, freedom of movement, and have forced us to weaken our immune systems by staying indoors. It is an abomination what each country has allowed to happen to its citizens. Here is a little fairy-tale for your consideration.

(Please note that the information below is merely fiction and not based on real people or real-life experiences and is merely served for entertainment purposes.)

Can you imagine the idiot who came up with this Covid-19? Imagine him standing in front of a room full of highly intelligent decision- makers and saying,

"Ladies and gentlemen, I present to you the Covid-19 pandemic virus. This is your opportunity to control your people without too much interference and get them to thank you while you control them. And this is how it will go down.

You will bombard your citizens with news about how to spot the virus, what it does, how it can affect you, symptoms to watch out for, how to prevent it, and most importantly, how seriously infectious the virus is. You need to tell them that it is in their own best interest to isolate for three months, yes, you heard me.

For three months, they must stay indoors, and not meet with other people (in case people start talking about what bullshit it is).

This in turn will also force them to watch the news with more interest to see how bad this virus is. Businesses will need to stop operating unless they can work from home, that is fine, because we have not thought about how we can force them not to work completely.

We must then wait for people to become desperate; they must be filled with fear. Once they are prepped with fear, then you tell them, do not worry, we have your backs, we will give you some money so you can feed your families. If you cannot pay your rent, do not worry, they cannot evict you, so you are ok. They cannot take away your car and household goods – yet. That will come later, don't tell them though. They must figure it out by themselves.

This will make them more willing to stay at home, and this in turn will weaken their immune system and cause possible anxiety, depression, and even lead to suicide.

Once your citizens are starting to cause riots and demanding that you open everything up, then warn them that the virus is still viral and can kill them and advise them that you need a little more patience before unlocking the country – remember to say it is for their greater good. Then release them and give them a little taste of freedom.

They will be so desperate for work that they will do anything you ask them to do. Give them a couple of months, and then do this all over again, but this time, shove the vaccine in their faces and threaten them with more poverty, alienation, and death if they do not take it. Keep your borders closed, track every person's movement and if they do not conform to your rules, take them out.

Ok, ok, I see you bending over with laughter at my invented fairy tale. All tales had a smidgen of truth to them and were elaborated to such an extent that no-one could take it seriously any longer.

So fine, let us tell another fairy tale.

The virus is real and deadly and we should stay inside to avoid it and don't forget those masks cause they do work don't they, oh no hold on, it is said that indeed it does not keep the virus out, but you should use one anyway because if you are ill, and you sneeze, you at least will get it all over your mask and not on other people.

I do not know how you were taught to sneeze, but we were shown to sneeze and cough on the inside of our arms – not on people!?

There is another theory that the world leaders know that society is waking up to how life is supposed to be, not how they have told us it should be. Time will tell though, and I am currently keeping my options open.

You see, you are the creator of your reality.

You control your life regardless of what other people say and do. No one can make you do anything. You do this all by yourself!

You allow everything that is in your life. You are the creator of all the magical and not so magical moments in your life. You created it, you allowed it in and made it real, so well done.

You are a perfect master manifestor.

Your power is enormous; you just do not know the sheer depth and magnitude of your power.

Claim the life you deserve!

CHAPTER TWENTY-FOUR
FEAR AND ANXIETY

I would like to share a couple of the techniques I use when I feel anxiety or fear overpowering me.

The first thing you need to do is become aware of it.

Quickly scan your memory bank to see if any real dangers are threatening your life this very minute.

If yes, phone the police immediately or phone a friend to come pick you up. If not, then start with a relaxing Chakra cleansing meditation.

I use this one at least once a week to stay grounded and keep my energy fields open.

Take a deep breath through your nose, count to six, hold for six, exhale to the count of six, and repeat it three times.

With your eyes still closed, feel your body relax as you imagine entering a beautiful nature reserve. You can feel the sun heating your skin and a cool refreshing breeze stroking your face.

You hear the birds chirping in the background and the sound of water running somewhere. You lie on the cool, crisp grass and place your hands on your Root Chakra (the area just above your public bone). The deepest colour of red streams in from the top of your head and flows warmly throughout your entire body.

See and feel the warmth of this beautiful red colour grounding you, feel mother earth and all her beautiful positive energy flowing through her and you. Now say the following:

"I am safe, I am secure, I am passionate, I am courageous and loved."
Take a deep breath in and out and relax.

A warm feeling of pure and unlimited joy fills your body as the most vibrant shade of orange fills your entire being.

A sudden burst of excitement wells up in your belly and while holding your hand over your Sacral Chakra (the area just below the navel) say, "I am a creative genius, I love my life and I find joy in the smallest of things." Take a deep breath in and out and relax.

While basking in the glow of orange, you see a bright beautiful yellow colour and a deep sense of belonging fills your entire being.

As the colour yellow covers you from head to toe, a bright sense of clarity pops in your mind and you are filled with wonder and awe at how amazing and worthy you are of receiving all you wish for.

Feel and see the yellow as you hold your hands over your Solar Plexus Chakra (the area just underneath your chest bone) and say, "I am worthy of receiving all the abundance in the universe. Anything I want, which is for my highest good and those around me, I can have – I am worthy of receiving it now."

Take a deep breath in and out – and relax.

While this beautiful colour is circling your body, you see the deepest shade of green entering your body. You can instantly feel your illnesses and pain fade away.

As if by magic, none of your old pain or discomfort is evident any longer – you can see a dark brown colour being washed away as the healing energy of green light takes its place. A warm and tingling feeling of love and compassion washes over you and you feel intense love for yourself and those around you. As this beautiful healing colour of green washes over you, you hold your hands over your Heart Chakra (your heart) and say, "I am a perfectly created being, worthy of love. I love myself and I have compassion for those around me."

Take a deep breath in and out – and relax.

As you lie there with a smile on your face a soft blue colour rushes over you. You instantly feel inspired to speak your truth.

A gentle feeling of peace and harmony engulfs your entire being as you put your hands over your Throat Chakra and speak the following words, "I speak my mind freely and God bless this energy field for the highest good and those that hear me."

Take a deep breath in and out – and relax.

The most beautiful indigo purple colour now fills your entire being and you feel your inner awareness opening. Your intuition has been activated and you can see your purpose clearly. As you hold your hands over your Brow Chakra (the space between your eyes), you whisper, "I now know my life's purpose and I am open to gaining new wisdom."

Take a deep breath in and out and relax.

Your entire being is vibrating with beautiful, positive energy and turns into a violet purple with flashes of bright white light in-between. You are feeling the presence of something very sacred inside your heart – engulfing you with so much love and gratitude for sharing this energy with you. As you hold your hands over your Crown Chakra (the area on top of your head), you thank the Universe for all the beauty and blessings it holds for you and say:

"I am now willing and open to receive all the abundance and wonder you have to offer me. Thank you."

Take a deep breath in and out and relax.

Set your intention for the day, whether you have an important meeting or a heavy workload – set your intention that it will be a productive day, that you will have infinite time to get everything done today, or your meeting will bear positive fruit.

There are thousands of guided meditations available on YouTube nowadays. It only needs to take 5-10 minutes and you will feel instant relief.

Try to always have soft meditation music playing in the background and don't engage in battles. Try to stay focused on your breathing throughout the day and make a list of all that you are grateful for.

It can honestly be anything, so long as you feel the gratitude for that said thing or person.

Think about something until you find a glimmer of joy or hope fluttering around, then build on that.

Hold on to that feeling for as long as you can. Do not let your mind wander and think about negative or bad things.

Stay away from social media and the news for the day and only read or watch positive movies or books. It is crucial not to fall into the familiar pit of self- pity and resentment. You must stay in control of your mind. You are the boss, not your mind.

You control your body, not the other way around. Tell your body and mind who is boss – you! I know the feeling comes and go in waves, but when I catch it on the low, and that familiar cold, gnawing fear tries to strangle me, I hold out and quickly think of something I am going to do later that day or the weekend that is kind of nice. For me, that would be baking with the kids or going for a walking the forest or meditating with my angels. You must find a few things you enjoy doing and keep it like bullets for your gun.

The bullets are the information you feed the gun (your fear). So, you need to make sure you always have ammunition handy to feed the gun. For example: If wake up feeling anxious and fearful.

I do my chakra cleansing and go for a walk. I remove myself physically from the place where I was feeling anxious.

When that pang of fear stabs my stomach again, I am ready.

I quickly tell myself, how excited I am to go on that walk or bake that delicious chocolate cake and I keep thinking of that fun thing I am going to do to convince my body that the feeling I just experienced was excitement and not fear. I do this over and over until the fear subsides. The truth is – and this is scientifically proven, your body does not know the difference between fear and excitement. It creates the exact same response in your body and it is up to your mind telling your body which one you are experiencing – so you can bullshit your body into believing it is excitement when you are actually fearful.

"Fake it till you make it," much.

It takes a while to get used to and you must become vigilant and watch your thoughts to not let them stray to negative worries again. You must curb it immediately and replace it with something positive. Eventually, after about a month you will see a difference in your levels of anxiety and the severity of your attacks.

Your thoughts are electricity and if you think the same thing over and over, it eventually creates or burns grooves in your brain.

It creates a path in your mind where your thoughts are created by thinking in a certain way. If you are not a deliberate creator then your mind will automatically take the route you carved for it previously and it will always lead down that same road.

That is why it is so hard in the beginning, to think in a new way, because your mind has not been exercised before and the only existing path is the one your lazy thoughts created. That is why you need to stay vigilant and steer your thoughts onto a new path so you can create a new highway in your mind
– but this time, one of positivity and prosperity. Stay on course, it does get easier I promise.

Remember to also keep that gratitude list or journal close by.

Keep adding to this list of things to be grateful for and before you know it, you will see more.

Most importantly, breath and just be gentle with yourself. Don't berate yourself and say horrible things about what you did wrong. Your body listens to your thoughts and the words you speak. So, make sure you say affirming and encouraging words to yourself. Because you are worth it!

Just keep practising and before you know it – you will see a brand new, better, improved, and happier you.

You have got this; you can do it – I promise you.

If I can do it, then you sure as heck can too. Big hug x

CHAPTER TWENTY-FIVE
MANIFESTATIONS

This is probably the most important lesson I have learned over the past year. To surrender and release or in other words - let go and trust. Put your order in with the universe, claim it, know it is yours, be grateful for what you do have, and then hand it over to the powers that be to help create the life you dream of. You are worth so much more than you think.

I have been an avid student of The Law of Attraction since I found my blissful experience with God / Source / The Creator.

I have been following Abraham Hicks, Wayne Dyer, Louise Hay, Joe Dispenza, and many others like them for the past few years and I can promise you it does get easier. My new favourite speaker, who I was recently referred to by my dear cousin, is Florence Scovel Shinn.

She wrote her first book, 'The Game of Life and How to Play It' in the 1920's – dear heavens, she was way ahead of her time!

I was fascinated by the idea that I could create my own life. It is very liberating, but at the same time, you must also accept the bad that you have allowed in your life and accept responsibility for that.

What I have learned over the past few years, is that old habits are hard to break. We have been hardwired to think a certain way.

To doubt, to fear, to think of ourselves as unworthy of receiving good things in life or that we are greedy for wanting a good life, or that we should just be grateful for what we do have.

I agree we should always be grateful for what we have, but we do deserve a great and happy life where all our dreams come true.

I learned that life is not here to punish us, it is here to be explored. Life is the most beautiful gift God has ever given us.

Everything just works and flows in the universe.

Everything is so intricately balanced and in harmony, what we need to do is just go with the flow, dream up our dreamy little life, inhale the feel-good emotion and simply know that it is on its way. It is that simple, but unfortunately, we get in our own way.

We ask for what we want, and then we start working on making it happen. Then low and behold if it does not come true the next week. We are so impatient and such little doubters, we never let go and trust that the Universe has our back, and so, things start falling apart. Please do not get me wrong, I still fall into this trap now and again. It is so incredibly challenging to stay positive and believe the unbelievable and that which you cannot see.

We like believing only once we see it, and now we are told we must believe it before it happens, and only then will it come true...

How? How are we supposed to do that? Well with a lot, and I mean a lot, of practice.

I listen to my teachers for at least an hour a day to stay upbeat and motivated and inspired.

It is hard to keep your focus positive and your emotions matching your dreamy future – but that is the secret.

Your emotions are the vibrations that send your wishes and dreams to the Universe and then that is what you get in return. So, if your emotions are of lack and doubt, then that is exactly what you will receive. That is why the teachers insist that you use the first 5 – 15 minutes every morning in meditation to help you start your day in the right and positive vibration to attract what you want.

I meditate every day for about 30 minutes, sometimes more and sometimes a little less, but every day I do this to keep my emotions in a good vibrational match to my dreams.

What I do, is make a small little area mine, where I burn my candle and incense sticks.

I keep my crystals close by and often clean them to clear away stagnant energies. I enjoy using my beautiful Tibetan singing bowl to start. My monkey mind is difficult to quieten, so it helps me focus on just creating the sweet sound.

I then pray for whatever is on my mind and thank them for all my blessings. Then, I dream up how I want my day to go or what my next big manifestation is. Once I am done, I keep my eyes closed and ask them if they have anything, they wish to tell me. I then wait to see if I hear or see anything in my mind's eye. When I am done, I give thanks again, blow out my candle and ring my bell to end off our conversation, then I am ready to take on the world.

I also do a cleansing ceremony every few months to rid the house and us of stuck and old negative energy. I spring clean the house while burning incense and open all the windows while playing energy clearing music. I burn candles and pray to my Angels and God to bless every part of the house and fill our home with love and peace. I write down everything that bothers me and then burn it while giving thanks for removing the obstacles from our lives.

I also write down my wish list for all the wonderful things I wish to enter my life and then give thanks as if I have already received it.

I wash my crystals often in sea salt and let them dry under the moonlight and the next day under the rays of the sun, so they are fully charged.

I also place special salts in the corners of the house to keep the positive energies alive in the house.

It is very liberating to do this cleanse when big changes have happened in your life.

What if doubt pours in?

It is so easy to get caught up in what is happening around you.

You see it on social media, the people around you and then you remind yourself that what you want is almost impossible to achieve. Then you start playing the "I'm not worth it" game. I didn't know that I do this until I beg Source to give me what I want. Then I would cry and say I know I am not worthy of receiving this, but I need it. I have done this so many times, I lost count.

Remember the hard wiring part. We are almost trained to believe that life must be hard, that we need to make a big sacrifice to fully enjoy life. This is so not true. Source does not want us to suffer!

He wants us to be joyful and have fun, to love life, and to surrender and release our fears and wants to Him. He knows exactly what we want, we have asked, now our job is to trust in His power and love to get that to us.

I have doubted the process so many times and then the self-blame would come, "Why don't you just believe? Why can't you just feel better? Why do you always have to doubt everything? Or even worse, you blame Source and stop believing that the process is working at all. You get so angry and feel stupid that you would believe in something that you cannot see. But then one morning you wake up and you get a warm feeling of love and joy fill your every being and you just know the day has arrived.

And then you get the call to say what you have been praying about for so long has arrived, just like that. Crazy.

I like to think of it as there are thousands of little universes out there. And every thought or wish of yours has launched a rocket and created that reality you wanted. So, there are hundreds and thousands of universes out there - in other words, different realities for our lives. We then need to simply focus on the life we do want and have unwavering faith that is the one we will be getting.

You need to push through the fear and know in your heart of hearts that what you wished for is coming to you.

Keep it to yourself, don't blab it out to everyone you know, because people love telling you how bad life is and how this one they know had such a bad life and this other one had a bad life and so it goes on and on until you are convinced that you are not worthy of receiving these wonderful gifts.

When you hang onto the faith and belief that you deserve the wonderful life you have asked for and get yourself ready to receive and live this great life, then it comes and the sweetness and bliss you experience from the gratitude of willing your new life into reality. Life is sweet and you deserve to live the new beautiful happy and blissful life you wished for.

CHAPTER TWENTY-SIX
TURNING 40

I had the privilege of turning 40-years in Scotland, surrounded by my beautiful children and husband. We broke those damn rules and had a picnic in one of the beautiful parks in Dunfermline. The forests are something to behold in this country. I honestly think this country has the prettiest forests in all the land.

I was more scared of turning 30 than 40, so that says something already. I am not someone that cares if you know my age, it is the most ludicrous thing to try and hide your age from others.

I am proud of every single wrinkle and grey hair on my head. My skin is not as beautiful and tight as it used to be and uh, my heavier bits are not as perky as they used to be, but I am ok with that. I love everything about my body. I love my feet and pretty toes (I am the only that thinks like this), I love my strong legs that walk me anywhere I want it to go. I love my bum and tummy, flabby and all, it is proof of the beautiful children I have borne. I love my chest, arms, neck, and my shoulders. I love my hands; I think they tell a story all on their own. I love my nails, the hair that grows on my body, the hair on my head, so lush with different shades of red, brown, and grey. I love my eyes, so big and inquisitive. I love my nose, smelling the pretty flowers in the garden. I love my teeth and my big smile. I love my little ears that can hear so well. I love my intestines, my kidneys, my lungs, my beautiful heart, and liver. I love my uterus and womb and I love my healthy blood, arteries, white cells, and my strong bones. I love my muscle (again, I am the only one that thinks I have muscles.) I love every freckle and imperfection on my skin. I love my mind, so electric and wonderful. There is not a thing I do not like about myself, well except my irritation. I get irritated if I do not get what I want as fast as I want it.

Try and see the best in yourself and others and soon that is all you will see.

CHAPTER TWENTY-SEVEN
MY LIFE'S PURPOSE REVEALED

I would like to share my vision / divine message with you.

I am not sure what to call it, but it came straight from God / Jesus / The Angels (one of them or all of them).

I have been instructed to share this message of hope and that is why you are reading this right now.

In a nutshell, I was promised safe passage to Scotland with my family, and in return The Angels want me to share my story.

For the past three years, I have been praying to God: "What is my Life's Purpose? Why am I here? Why have I undergone all these challenges and blessings? How can I be of service?"

Two weeks before we left for Scotland, I was meditating again, begging God and my Angels to help me find calm and peace.

My body was in a constant state of shock and fear. I think the word I am looking for is – in a state of terror. My heart would be racing, my body would go ice cold and then I would get dizzy with fear. My stomach was in a constant knot with that dreaded feeling of impending doom following me around.

Every part of my body would recoil with pain and discomfort, I was terrorized. I begged them: "I need your help. I am so scared; I don't know what to do.

Please tell me what to do."

I would normally feel calm and centred afterwards, but this time, something else also took place. I heard them say the following to me: "Stop worrying, you are going to get safe passage. Everything is working out for you. You are safe, this is in our hands now."

I burst into tears upon hearing these words and I just knew it was them. I saw them in my mind's eye laughing and dancing and so incredibly happy. It almost looked like they were poking fun at me and saying: "Don't stress you silly sausage, we have got this, relax, everything is working out for you!"

I was overcome with intense gratitude and excitement, I could not believe that they made me this promise and I didn't know how they were going to make it happen, but I just knew it was them.

I then heard: "Your duty is to share your story. You must become a beacon of light and help people find theirs. This is your Life's Purpose." I had been asking for so long what my Life's Purpose was, and they just simply said: "This is your Life's Purpose. Nothing can stop you. All of this had to happen exactly as it did and now you must share your story with the world."

As I finished my prayers, I drew my Angel card, and it was:

Spread Your Wings:

"Archangel Ariel: "Do not hold back right now. The timing is perfect, and you are ready to soar! Although you may feel intimidated by the prospect of change, and by the thought of moving past your comfort zone, you are ready to fly high. Welcome new opportunities and know that it is safe to follow your heart and dreams. Keep your focus upon love, service, and spirit, and avoid naysayers and sceptics. Remember that you inspire others with your story of turning challenges into victories."

Can you imagine receiving this message after hearing the message from my angels in my head?

There is always a little niggling voice in your head doubting yourself. Is this real? Did I hear that? How are the Angels going to make this happen? Who am I to want these things? Am I worthy of receiving all these blessings? What is so special about me?

What if this was all an illusion and we have nowhere to go?

But this card sealed the deal for me. And I just knew I had to surrender and release the situation to God and my Angels, and they will sort it out. I had to let go of control and trust 100% in their power. I had to break the earthbound rules and obey the law of Source. I had to trust and let go.

I hope you do not think of me a complete loon, I want to say, that I do not really care, but there is a small part of me that does care.

I do not think I even told my friends or family about this.

I would not say I am embarrassed; it is more the thought that they will perhaps think I am crazy and making things up. It was such a beautiful and special message and it was mine, delivered to me by these beautiful entities who simply want to love me and make me happy. They are mine. It was my little secret, our little thing. I would often talk to them about it. I even created a beautiful promise/vision board and included the writing symbol on it.

I would sometimes wake up in the middle of the night and think I need to finish this book. I made a promise.

But the writing was part painful, part therapeutic.

It helped me to find clarity, peace and forgiveness for myself and others. I was trying to stall for some time as I was scared to put it all out there, but I finally submitted my manuscript to a few publishing houses in July. A month ago, I received two offers from them, but I felt that I was not going to have the freedom to market my book the way I wanted to, so I declined their offers and started investigating self-publishing.

I am so thankful I went this route as it gave me the freedom to choose what my book will look like and control how it is marketed.

I hope you have enjoyed the book thus far and I would like to thank you for taking the time to read my story.

I truly hope that you will find your purpose, your magic - and never forget how incredibly special you are.

I would like to end off my book with the 40 life lessons I learned over my "young" life.

CHAPTER TWENTY-EIGHT
LIFE-LESSONS

Sometimes we can learn from other's mistakes. I hope you can take a few lessons from mine and they will spare you a few.

1. My opinion of you is none of your business.
This is such a big one for me. I used to care so much about what other people thought of me. I would get anxious at the thought that I was not considered good enough, or pretty enough or clever enough or cool enough. It used to drive me crazy! Now, I know I am good, clever, pretty, and cool – I am enough for myself and that is all that matters.

2. Trust your instincts.
You know exactly what to do. I used to go to everyone and ask them for their opinions and advice. Deep down I knew the answer, but I did not trust myself enough to go with my gut. Now when I want answers to questions, I go quiet and listen to the voice inside of me, the one that makes me feel good and eases the tension out of the question, then, I know that is the answer.

3. Not everyone is going to like you.
I used to be a people pleaser, I needed people to like me, it was like a drug. Now I understand that I am not everyone's cup of tea.
I am a little bit off, weird, loud, and crazy and I do not take offence if you do not like me. Imagine if we were all the same, how boring would that be, you are the spice – so be proud of who you are – curls, freckles and all.

4. People that anger you are there to teach you a lesson.
What you don't like in someone, is a hidden aspect inside yourself that you dislike. That person you so intensely dislike is there to teach you a lesson about yourself. It is hard to try and see it like this, but I

have come to some painful self-realisations by looking at the person I despise through compassionate eyes.

Brace yourself, this is a big one, but once you have this one under your belt, you will find fewer people like this crossing your path. If you don't, the situation or type of person will keep on appearing in your life until you have accepted that part of yourself, then forgive and love yourself all the more after recognizing that part of you.

5. You have the power to create your life and reality.
My thoughts and belief systems become my reality. When I thought I was unworthy of receiving good things in life, life threw hard things my way. Once I realised how amazing I am and how worthy I am of receiving love and happiness, I was showered by beautiful, positive experiences. You become your thoughts and beliefs and the beauty is, a thought can be changed. It starts with you. Become a deliberate creator. What do you want to create in your life? Think in that direction and work towards that goal and do not allow the old, negative, and lazy way of thinking to override your new positive trail of thoughts. It is not easy, I know. But practice does make perfect, so keep practising and if you fail, acknowledge it and say, tomorrow is a new day to start all over again and then tomorrow, try again and again until you have perfected your art of becoming a deliberate creator.

6. God is part of you, and you are part of the Creator.
I was brought up staunch Christian, you had to pray through Jesus to reach God as you were too unimportant to pray directly to God. It used to make me feel small and insignificant. Now I know that God is inside of me and I am directly linked to the energy of love. The love is so powerful and encompassing, I am co-creating my life with the awesome Creator of worlds. Our planet is created with such perfection and balance, everything is created to provide us with abundance and harmony. We are all linked together by the invisible energy that created us. Can you see the air that you breathe in? No?
But you can breathe otherwise you would be dead. Life is a game, and we need to learn to play it with love and intention.

7. An angry person is just someone that was deeply hurt.
Anger stems from unresolved pain and frustration. When you have been deeply hurt and had no way of dealing with the pain, it can either turn into depression or anger. I learned to turn to anger and it saved me from devastation. But at some point, you need to deal with that hurt, acknowledge it, accept it for what it was, and let it go. It will keep coming back to you until you have learned the lesson you were meant to learn and moved on. Anger can also become addictive. It empowers you

and shields you from what is happening underneath the surface – you do not deal with it because your anger creates that warm feeling of self-righteousness. But, if you never deal with why you became so angry, eventually you will die of a heart attack or brain haemorrhage. On the other hand, people also tend to stay away from you as your anger scares them and they would rather not confront you in case they get hurt. So, in the end, you sit and nurture that anger and think how wonderful and safe it is. How comforting it is. But it will kill you in the end.

8. Education is your best weapon.
We have become lazy to educate ourselves properly. Everything is spoon-fed to us daily, from what to eat, how to dress, what to believe, and even who you are. We need to start educating ourselves. Research facts, ask questions, and do not be afraid to look stupid. Knowledge from education is something no one can take away from you, you will always have it. Look for ways to further your education and you will be amazed how easy and affordable it is.

9. We are all equal.
No one is more important than you. Just because they have a position of power or live in a bigger house than you, does not make them better than you. Never think of yourself a lesser of a person just because you do not have wealth or a degree behind your name. We must all make use of the toilet and get naked when we shower, and we all must die. No one is taking their 'stuff' with them after death.

10. Know your worth.
Damn this one is so important. No person, place, or thing has the power to make you feel a certain way. You alone have the power to allow them to assert their power over you or not. You have the power to say, "No, I do not allow you to make me feel unworthy, stupid, or sad." Only you have the power to make yourself feel anything. It does not matter if you are in prison or living a shitty life. You still have the power to think positive thoughts and feel happy, just as you are intended to be.

11. Saying no is not a swearword.
You do not have to do everything people ask of you. We allow people to guilt us into their demands, but it is ok to say no if you do not feel like doing it.
There are way too many pressures put on us daily to do things that we do not want to do. You are not here to please everyone; you are here to play the game of life – so play it. Learn to listen to that little voice inside of you – when it tells you that it is tired and does not feel like going

out tonight. Do not worry about upsetting others. You need to rest and recover so that you can have the energy to do what is right for you.

12. Not everything is about you.
We are all in love with ourselves. It is masked in many ways, but deep down inside, we thrive on attention and need love like we need air. We think the universe revolves around us, and maybe it does, but not everyone's actions or words are about you. So many times, we walk into a shop and feel insecure about ourselves, thinking that people are judging us on how we look, the way we walk or talk, or who we are seen with. Most of the time, people simply do not care, they are too busy thinking that you are judging them. So, if you hear someone laugh as you walk past them, just chill – it is not about you.

13. Do not allow others to shame you into action.
I struggled with this one for an awfully long time. It is when we feel uneasy about an act or feeling that is deemed improper or ridiculous – according to society. I say Fuck that! You should never feel bad about being different or saying something ridiculous. This is one of the main reasons I started drinking. I was an oddball and did not fit in 100% anywhere. I was behaving improperly and said ridiculous things – all because I was different, and society tried to shame me. Don't allow them to shame you for being you. Learn to become your own best friend.

14. Rather do something and ask for forgiveness, than not do it at all.
If you think back on all the things you have done and have not done, which ones do you regret the most? The ones you did not have the courage or time to do? Yes, I have regrets for things I have done, but almost 99.9 % of the time, I am glad I did them. Sometimes we want to do something so badly and then we wait for permission – and sometimes that day just never comes. I believe in rather doing something and asking for permission afterwards, than asking for permission first and never end up doing it. Permission also comes from you by the way...

15. Time is your most precious commodity.
You can always make your money back, but you can never get your passed time back. Those clicking seconds are gone. What have you done with this precious gift? I cherish my time more than money. If you ask me for my time, you ask for a piece of me that I can never get back again. So value your own time and of those around you. Be present when you are speaking to someone, put that phone away and give them your undivided attention. Don't squander your precious commodity by

doing ten things at once. At the end of your life, you won't say, I wished that I spent more money on things. You would say, I wished I spend more time doing what I love and with those I love. Choose spending your time wisely.

16. Choose your life partner carefully.
I have seen so many people going through a divorce, it is now more common to be divorced than to still be together. We meet our special person, fall head over heels in love, and decide to get married for life. I never understood the rush. Why do you feel compelled to get married a mere eight months after you meet? You do not even know yourself; how can you even begin to comprehend who that person is? Does he/she make you laugh, put your needs first, communicate with you, share their most trusted secrets with you and encourage you to become a better person? Just remember that good looks will fade and all you will have in the end is each other's company. Compassion, communication, and respect are essential to the happiness of any relationship.

17. Going into a partnership is like marriage.
I had so many partnerships in business and I wish I knew then what I know now. I learned that you must check out the person you want to go into partnership with. Get references from people they have done business with.
Draw up a Memorandum of Agreement before you start the business, even if it is a joint venture.
Make sure both have signing rights when you open the bank account, not only one of you. Make sure each person's rights and responsibilities are clearly outlined, defined, and agreed upon before commencing and with monthly KPI's (key performance indicators) to make sure it is all in progress. You should both have something of value that you bring to the table, otherwise you can just get an employee to fulfil the function. Do not get someone that is just like you. You need a yin for your yang, a conservative person if you are rash or an analytical person if you are creative.

18. Money is just energy.
I was brought up with, "Does money grow on trees? Do I look like an ATM to you? Money is the root of all evil. They are mean because they have too much money – don't be like that."
It has only been three years since I learned that money is simply energy. If you think money is evil and hard to come by, then that is exactly what it will be for you. On the other hand, if you treat money with respect, always chase up what is owed to you, pay your debts with love, and know, how easy it is to bring into your life, then that is exactly

what it will be for you. I always make sure I have money in my wallet and a little card that says: "I always have enough. Money keeps flowing into my bank account. I am safe."

19. It is ok to just do nothing.
I was indoctrinated that I must always be busy. As children, we always made sure we looked busy when we were at home or else someone would find something for us to do. Society also builds on the perception that busy people are successful people. It is so 1980. Busy is just that – busy. Just because you are always busy does not make you successful, worthy, or a better person. It doesn't mean you are getting things done. I have since discovered that I get more things done when I am doing nothing.... How? You ask. Because when I do nothing, I relax, and when I am relaxed, I am more inclined to dream and be creative, and during this process, I find answers to all my problems or simply see them for what they are – just made up problems. I love the Abraham Hicks saying: "There is nothing serious going on here." And so, I often just do nothing and find the most incredible solutions and creative ideas being born from here.

20. Others cannot make you happy – only you can do this.
If you wait for something or someone to make you happy – you will have an exceptionally long wait ahead of you. I think this is the reason most marriages fail – your partner expects you to make them happy and this is impossible. Only you can make yourself happy. Happiness is a choice. Every morning you wake up, you decide if you want to be happy or miserable – and then so it is.

21. Meditation is key to a healthy mind, spirit, and body.
I hated the idea of meditating. I considered it boring and a waste of my time. How am I supposed to still my mind? Today, I would be lost if I did not meditate daily. I can feel the difference if I have not meditated for one day – I feel grumpy, irritable, and just out of sorts. Meditation is the art of quieting your mind. You can do it from anywhere and it costs absolutely nothing.

22. Your past does not define you.
For too long I believed that I am defined by my past. I have felt inadequate because of where I came from or for being poor at times. I remember at one stage when I was in primary school, my father was made redundant and we were living on welfare. I did not know it and fought with my teacher one day about something silly – "my rights versus the law". I said something like, "My parents are paying for us to be in this school and it is our right to have this." My sister heard, took

me aside, and told me that we were on welfare. It shamed me to my core. I felt so humiliated and unworthy – which of course is ridiculous (wealth does not define you) and since then I became demure and just kept quiet at school.

What I am trying to tell you is that it doesn't matter where you are from, if you were poor or rich, black or white, gay or straight, man or woman – it does not define you. Your character does. What sort of person you are, how you think, speak, and act – this defines who you are. So be proud of what a beautiful, special human being you are – you only get one life – live it! There is only one of you – enjoy being unique!

23. Exercise is more important for your psyche than your body.
When I arrived in the Netherlands, I was incredibly depressed. I felt guilty about how I had left my country. All I wanted to do was clean, I could not clean enough. My house was sparkling and then that happened to be the only job I could get too, so I became a professional cleaner and I loved it. When your soul is at dis-ease, you try all sorts of things to make it go away. Under normal circumstances, I would have drunk it away, but since that was no longer an option – I cleaned and cleaned until I would have nothing left inside of me.

This exercise helped me more than I ever thought possible. I felt like I physically purged the old, stale energy inside of me and the deep breathing from the exercise rejuvenated my body and soul.

24. Excitement and fear create the same reactions in your body.
I was overcome by irrational fear when I moved to the Netherlands. That gnawing in the pit of my stomach was killing me. It gave me an ulcer and weakened my body, mind, and spirit. You cannot live in fear and be prosperous. I tried everything to overcome this fear. I would spring-clean till my body ached. I would meditate till I fell asleep. I would listen to podcasts on how to turn negative emotions into positive ones. I went back to taking my sleeping tablets and hoped I would wake up feeling better. I did lots of cuddles with the kids and went for long walks in nature, and that helped me a lot. But then I heard the podcast about how fear and excitement are the same response in your body, it is your mind that tells you whether it is supposed to be good or bad and that was it for me.

25. No-one can make you feel inferior without your consent.
This is another huge lesson I have learned. No-one can make you feel stupid, inferior, worthless, or ugly, unless you allow them to. People treat you the way you allow them to treat you. I know it is difficult, but with enough practice, you will get there. Just always remember this. When someone treats you with disrespect, speak up immediately

and say something like, "I do not appreciate how you just spoke to me. If you can not address me in a respectable manner, then please do not speak to me at all." They will quickly learn that you will not accept them being rude to you anymore and see how their attitude towards you change.

"You can't change the people around you, but you can change the people around you." – Unknown.

26. If you don't like where you are – move. Simple.

I never understood people who would lament their terrible lives and keep repeating it over and over until it became their mantra. If you do not like the way your life is going, you hate your job, feel stuck in a relationship or you hate the way you look – then change it. It starts by making the decision to make a change and then setting up goals on how to achieve it, and every day taking a little step (no matter how small) towards realising your dream. I promise it is not so hard. It is one of the easiest things in life to do, but it starts with you deciding to make that choice, believing that you are worthy of that change, and then accepting it when it comes into your life. You are worthy!

"If you don't like how things are, change it! You're not a tree." - Jim Rohn

27. Your family is not only blood, but they are also the ones that are here to teach you a life lesson.

I believe that we choose our parents and the life we are born into. I think what we struggle with is the bond of blood we share with our family, but what we forget is the energetic bond we share with all living creatures. We are ultimately all family and connected by our consciousness as one. I believe our family serves as either our support or the major life lessons we need to learn. We all come to earth to overcome an important life lesson and transcend. Your family is normally your pack who decided to come to earth together and help each other achieve our life's purpose. So, if your family members hurt you deeply or cause you major frustration, then it is time to think about what life lesson they are here to teach you. Don't you find it strange how estranged family members wind up together or meet at a bizarre place to reignite their connection and forgive each other? Love your family and thank them for the role they have played in helping you reach your highest form.

28. We are meant to thrive and not only survive.

I sometimes still go into fits of rage when I think how the system has enslaved us to our poverty mindset. We have been trained from a young age that nothing comes without suffering. Take our beautiful Jesus – our magical, kind, loving, gentle Jesus.

He came to teach us about love and kindness and how to live from Source within. He taught us that we have everything we need already inside of us; all we need to do is ask and believe it to be so and it will be. He taught us about caring for others, that only love is real and that it does not matter if you are a prostitute or a king, you are all equally important of the love of God. People and society have distorted his truth into making us believe that we must suffer and punish ourselves to find peace. We have been taught that we must suffer to achieve our goals, that life is not supposed to be easy, and we must fight for what we have – the survival of the fittest and all that. It still gives me the chills how we have been brainwashed into this limited way of thinking. It is only once we are free from the shackles of our limited self-beliefs that we see the truth and beauty of Jesus' teachings. We are meant to thrive and not merely survive.

29. Having fun in life is more important than anything else.
When last did you do something fun or laugh till your belly-ached? Can you remember the euphoria and lightness you experienced afterwards? – the afterglow so to speak. This is what life is supposed to be like for you all the time. Life is just a game. You are here to play it and to bend those stupid man-made rules and live by the rules of Source only. You are not meant to be contained – you are so much more than you think you are. Your spirit is seeking freedom and to live life to the fullest. Do you not see this precious gift you have been given? To live this life on earth, to explore and expand your body, mind, and soul. Make more time to go out and have fun, be happy, and experience love and joy!

30. Find a hobby outside of work
You might find the older you get, the less time or interest you have in hobbies. We tend to be consumed by work and then the little time we have left we throw toward our family and friends. How are we supposed to have time for a hobby? Well, the same way you did when you were younger. The time when you cared about your happiness, when you wondered how life worked and where you fitted into the picture. Life is all about balance and if we pour all our time and energy into only work, what will be left of us when one day we are without work? Find a hobby, something you look forward to doing and nourish and grow that. One day it will stand you in good stead.

31. Addiction is part of a stuck emotion
I would say 90% of all addictions stem from a traumatic experience or recurring negative emotions you have not dealt with. If you are brave

enough, you can overcome your addiction by facing what happened to you, acknowledging it, forgiving yourself or the person and letting it go. Find something wholesome to fill the hole. I rediscovered God and my Angels through meditation and that is still my guiding light when I feel like giving up. When dealing with an addiction you must have been told numerous times that your sobriety is the most important thing in the world. Protect yourself from falling into old habits and be selfish. You are number one.

32. Believe in magic.
It breaks my heart when I see all the sadness and hurt around me. There is so much magic around us, we just need to accept the truth of magic and it will become real. We find ourselves stuck, staring at the stupid reality in front of us, and we forget that we created this reality. The way we are made is pure magic, how our bodies function, how the world spins on its axis, how earth gives us oxygen, and how it is connected to the trees, the animals, the moon and the sun – it is ALL magic!! Please do not stop believing in the magic just because you cannot see it right now. Keep looking at the magic that is around you and soon that is all you will see.

33. Listen to the advice you give others, as it applies to you too.
Ooh, I am at fault here... I love dishing out advise and then not taking it myself... You will soon find how accurately that advice applies to you. So next time you advise others, perhaps record it, and keep it for later, for yourself.

34. Find something to be grateful for every single day.
I fell into a deep depression a few times, and during all those times I had forgotten to stay grateful for what I had. I would only long for what I did not have and see the lack rather than all the abundance that I already had around me. I now consider being grateful as important as breathing and do it every single morning, before I open my eyes – I think of all the wonderful things I am grateful for. Sometimes there is not a lot I can think of and then I focus on nature. I think how happy it makes me seeing a sunset or sunrise, or hear the birds chirping outside, or the wind rustling through the trees while I am cuddled in my nice warm bed, or I think about seeing the dolphins jumping in and out of the ocean or spotting an unusual animal such as a deer, tortoise or eagle in my path.
Just learn to be more grateful and you will find more things to be thankful for every day.

35. Letting go of control allows things to happen.

Mm... I hear you. Yes, it is h-a-r-d! I am a control freak and learning to let go was, is, and probably always will be something I need to remind myself of constantly to keep my sanity. I want everything and I want it, yesterday! I am so impatient, I want to mould things into perfection, to the exact specs I demand, right now! And then, I get furiously frustrated when this is not happening, and I say to God, "Why did you take your light off me? I worked so hard for this, why am I not getting it?" And then He says – "Just breathe" I listen, and breathe, and all expectations just fall away, and I surrender. A few days later, just when I have almost forgotten about what I was so hastily in need of, it arrives perfectly and most unexpectedly. Gloriously, perfectly balanced, and on time. So next time you are anxiously trying to make things fit, just stand back, take a deep breath, and let go. I love you; I know it is hard, but it tastes so sweet when it does arrive.

36. We all have something truly remarkable and special inside of us. We are all created in the image of God's perfection. We are beautiful and perfect. It does not matter if you are round, short, tall, speckled, and freckled – you are simply perfect, and you have a divine purpose to fulfil on this earth. Source does not make mistakes and you sure as heck are not a mistake. You chose this life and the body you are in – find your purpose and live it with confidence and joy. In all my time that I have mentored people, I have yet to find one that is useless. Every single one of us has something unique and special inside of us that will set us up on our path. It is your job to find that oyster, and when you find that spark and feel the fluttering in your stomach, then you are well on your way to finding your purpose.

37. Our life's purpose is to be joyful.
I might sound like a stuck record, but it is true, and when this truth has been denied for so long it becomes harder to hear and believe. So just one more time in case you did not get it the first 100 times, you are meant to be joyful! Your life is meant to be easy and joyous, prosperous, and abundant. You are meant to thrive and explore life. You are meant to be happy and to be loved. If you are none of these things, you need to relook at your life and make changes.

38. Rather try and fail, than not try at all.
I take my hat off to the millions of people who at least try to better themselves, get a better job, start that business, start walking to lose that weight, or ask the person they like out on a date. It starts with a flash feeling, an excitement, an idea and then you have two choices – 1. Ignore the feeling or thought, or 2. Act out on the thought or idea. What do you have to lose?

Want a raise or promotion? Just ask. Want to go on a date with that cute guy or pretty girl? Just ask. Want to lose 5kg? Start walking. Just start somewhere. If you break up your goal into little bite-size chunks, then it is more manageable. Every day you can tackle one aspect of it, and before you know it, one hundred days will have gone by and you have achieved your goals! My father always said to me: "Just ask! What have you got to lose? The worst that can happen is they say no. But what if they say yes? So just ask and see what happens – they can only say no."

39. Stay away from negative people.
Choose your battles and stay away from energy vampires. They always have a problem for every solution. You do not need to fight everyone. In life, I have found that people just react to everything thrown their way. If something bad or unexpected happens to us, we feel like we need to react to it immediately. But not every battle presented to you is worth your time and energy. Some people just enjoy getting a rile out of you and will do anything in their power to get a reaction. Do not let them. Do not become part of their drama. Some people thrive on drama and look for the rush. They always seek something to complain about or tell sad stories about. They thrive on your energy and will suck it from you until there is nothing left. You know, the ones who ask the same question over and over, every week, month, or year, and you keep giving them the same advice. I call them 'Askholes' - Like an asshole, asking all the time, so I coined it - an 'Askhole'. I did warn you; I am not the nicest person around... Whatever you do, do not indulge them by joining in on the complaining session. I know it is tempting and sometimes it is nice to just complain about something with someone. If you must, then just say, "Ok, we have 5 minutes to lament the woes of the world, complain, and then, it's over." Set your alarm and stick to it, and then change the subject to something positive immediately after.

40. Rules are meant to be broken.
Ah, my favourite! I love breaking rules. I honestly believe that rules are simply created to be broken. My Acudetox trainer said that people who had no boundaries when they were younger are bound to end up in trouble with the law. It upset me because I believe it is yet another rule that has been placed upon us. Don't push too far, stay in your lane. You see, rules are basic guidelines to get people to tow-the-line, to keep them feeling uninspired and insignificant. Once you break those rules, you see they are simply there to keep us dumb and controlled. Please do not get me wrong, I am not saying go and break the law by stealing, murdering, or speeding, etc. When I say break those damn rules – I mean the rules that you and society have placed upon yourselves.

We must break the chains of enslavement and free ourselves from the shackles of the prison in our minds. Our mind is our most powerful weapon. It can help us achieve anything we want. If the will is there, you WILL find a way. Ask, believe it is so, and it will be. Break those DAMN rules you placed upon yourself. Say, "No more! I deserve more! I am free! I am worthy! I am powerful! I am beautiful! I am perfect in every way! I am smart! I am loveable! I am kind! I am at peace! Things always work out for me! I am healthy! I am energetic! I am creative! I am blessed! I am love! I can do and be anything! I am part of God and He is part of me. I am truth! I am prosperous! I am wealthy! I am joyful! I am free to think and be whomever I choose to be!"

NOW GO HOME
LITTLE ONE

The time has come for me to release you from your obligations, little one. I can no longer carry your fears and doubts with me.
Last night, you came to me in tears, begging me not to release this book into the big bad world.
You told me you fear being hurt again, and that people will make fun of you. You told me I must rather hold on to it and that it was enough just to write it. It served its original intention, to purge and rid us of your stuck emotions, but now you are trying to hold me back little one.
I cannot let you control me anymore. I am a grown woman.
I have experienced it all with you and held your hand throughout.
I cuddled you and laughed with you and kept the light on while you were sleeping.
I have been guarding you and protecting you all this time, but it is now time for me to step into my light.
I must do this, for both of us.
If I walk away now, I will forever be in your shadows. I love you more than words can ever express.
We are one and the same.
Your blood is mine, my eyes are yours, we share the same heart, we will forever be the same, but I cannot be scared anymore.
I cannot let your fears and insecurities overshadow my longing for release any longer.
It is time for you to step into my shadows and let me run the show. I will never leave you – I promise.
I will never be far away.
I want you to go and play with your favourite dolls, build sandcastles, and laugh until your belly hurts.
You are my inner child, I am your parent, and I need to parent you now.
We will still have fun together and do silly things.
I will always look out for you and protect you from danger. But I cannot cower and hide behind you any longer.

I release you, to be the light, to live a care-free life – safe in the knowledge that Spirit and I have got your back.
We are one and the same and you are safe dear one. I love you. Go and be a child, while I do this thing called life.
I need to put my big-girl panties on now and be strong.
I cannot have you temper me with irrational fears and what-ifs.
I am also learning to be brave and have the courage to stand up for what I believe in.
I too am scared.
But I have got to at least try.
Please understand, I am not angry with you. You have done nothing wrong little one.
You have always been and will always be my source of inspiration. I admire you for getting dressed each day and going to work and dealing with people as if you were their peer.
But you are not.
You are just a scared little girl, pretending to be someone you are not meant to be.
But you do not have to do this anymore.

Thank you for trying every single day.
For trying to be brave and for looking out for me.
I needed you more than I realised, but it is time to let you go now, so you can be free and learn to be a child again, while I get on with preparing us for our next stage.
I have got this.
Do not fear, do not be sad, I am always just a small little tug away.

Love you, always,
Grown-up You xxx"

> Stay blessed and always remember how
> very precious and powerful you are!
> Thank you for reading.

Printed in Great Britain
by Amazon